Close Encounters with God

Big and Little Miracles

By

Kathleen McLaughlin

Dedicated to

Seekers of the True and Living God

Table Of Contents

Preface

Before anything else, I want to credit those who helped me
with this book. Each principal character in the stories was
key in making sure the stories were accurate and well told.
Francie Baron was a huge help in editing and rewriting,
along with my readers, Bill Abel, Gail Pazdur, Shelly
Rosenberg, and Marcie Marshall. My husband Lee allowed
me to bounce ideas off him and was the go-to guy for all the
self-publishing. Much work and patience has been required
of each contributor, so I would like to share credit for the
writing with each of those who labored with me.

This work was a work of love for all involved--intended to
help, to heal, to bless, to increase hope and faith, and to aid
with the daily choices that create and build our character.
We can grow and change with God's help— His miracles
can be great catalysts in doing that.

Writing this book has been a wonderful experience for me,
totally changing my point of view on many things. My belief
now is that everyone has a story to tell (probably along with
some miracles to recount from their lives)—it just takes
eyes, ears, and hearts opening to reveal it.

As I heard about some of the gut-wrenching life events in
these stories, I was struck by the fact that humility and
courage are required to accept that there is a greater power
than us who can be involved in our lives. Yet, it is even
more frightening to think that we might be alone, and that no
one is guiding the universal wheel. If humankind and
creation are just happenstance, then we truly are on a lonely
and pointless journey. These stories show just the
opposite—there is a loving and very personal God who will
do life with us if we just ask and follow his lead. Our lives,

in concert with Him, can have eternal meaning and treasures.

It has been such a privilege to have griefs, triumphs, and adventures of others shared with me. A renewed respect for the perseverance, resilience, and love in those around me has been a byproduct of those stories for me. My eyes, ears, and heart have been renewed to truly see, hear, and love people because of the narratives these dear people have poured out.

Furthermore, each story gave me some insight into ways that I want to revamp my thoughts, words, and actions. As is evident in these tales, true transformation comes through a joint effort with the Holy Spirit. This is not a self-help book—it is about collaborative effort in concert with the Helper.

As each story landed in my heart, I found myself looking for common elements in the stories. What enabled these people to have faith, to trust God, to persevere through the ordeals, and to stay hopeful through to the end? It resonates with me and my own experience that this happens one choice at a time. God stays with us, but as we can choose trust, hope, and faith during difficult times, we build more faith muscles to believe, hope, and trust increasingly on a day-to-day basis. That opens our abilities to cooperate with God as He works miracles. The miracles almost always end in ways to pay it forward, to help others (often in the same areas that we have lived through trials).

Lastly and greatly, writing this collection of stories has reopened the eyes of my heart to see how much God listens, sees, and responds to us. We have a God who truly loves us—He pursues us and never leaves us to do life on our own, unless that is what we desire.

Now, let me tell you a little about the McLaughlin family, so that our tales (interspersed among the other narratives) come to life a bit more as you read them. Of course, these descriptions barely scratch the surface.

Lee is the gentle giant and the glue to our family. At six foot and five inches, Lee is a big man with a huge, loving heart. He is extremely slow to take offense and careful with his words. Lee is the kindest person I have ever known. As one whom people seek out for wisdom or advice, he is in high demand. Our boys often ask for his counsel, but even relative strangers seem to recognize his wisdom. Currently, Lee, who had a career as an engineer, is turning into a passionate teacher. He bursts out into teaching mode in various situations, leaving the privileged listeners a little richer for the hearing.

As wife and mother, I, (Kathy) have always been the more highly-strung one. My greatest gift as a mom was the talent of snuggling. I am convinced that cuddling and praying have covered a multitude of my sins as a mother and wife. My heart's desire as a mom has always been for our whole family to be part of the kingdom of God. It has not yet come completely to pass. In my older years, I am experiencing an increased sense of urgency to let people know about God's love.

Starting at the age of fifty-three, I have had three, separate and distinct cancers and have existed with a slow-growing lymphoma for almost one and a half decades. Living through these has changed my life for the better in many ways. It has given me a more eternal perspective and an empathy that had been sorely lacking in me.

A reality that I have discovered in my later life is that pain and suffering can be a good thing, shaking us out of lethargy and onto a better path, if we so choose. The narratives in this book helped me to see a correlation between pain and growth even more clearly. They have also assisted me in seeing how much we can be enriched by each other's stories.

Tim, as our oldest son, has been focused and determined from birth. A leader and a forger of new ways of thinking or doing, Tim is driven. He loves intensely but keeps his feelings tightly under wraps.

Patrick is our diverse son, with talents in many areas. With an ability to analyze quickly and to see below the surface of events and situations, Patrick has always been a solution finder. He works at a think tank and is loaded with brain power but spreads his interests into music, nature, and sports. Patrick feels richly but tends to keep lots hidden in the deep waters of his heart.

Kevin is no less amazing, with powerful people skills along with an ability to drill down to what people really need. He listens and hears with his heart. Kevin's hallmark is gentleness and kindness, yet he can hold his own when a confrontation is needed. He has chosen to follow in Lee's footsteps in both his career and his philosophy on life.

All the guys are very family oriented, with high priority on being good fathers and husbands. We are a blessed family with our share of strengths, weaknesses, flaws, and heartaches, some of which you may see throughout the book.

Introduction

What Is a Miracle?

This book is about so much more than mere stories of miracles. It applies examples of miracles to our lives and attempts to answer questions about what miracles mean to us personally. What is the purpose of miracles? How do they change us? Can we truly be an active part of a miracle ourselves? Do they make a difference for eternity? Do we even recognize the miracles as they happen around us? Can we be trained to have open spiritual eyes and ears so that we can see and hear in the spiritual realm? Can miracles happen to non-believers as well as to Christians? Are miracles everyday occurrences? Can miracles be much more than just cool things that show there is a God? Could they be God's way of talking to us? Of showing Himself and His character? Could they be testaments of God's great love for us? Can miracles sometimes lurk underneath the most tragic events? Let's look for the answers in these true-life stories.

Historically in the Judeo-Christian community, miracles have been viewed differently than the approach in this book. This work is about miracles that are part of ordinary people's regular lives, both large and small. It describes miracles that we all might see in our lives if we ask for God's help in perceiving them. In the premise of this writing, miracles are simply our interactions with God.

A miracle is an event in which you see God's hand, his interventions, his assistance, his details, his plan, or his protection. With a true miracle, you will witness a profound change because the Holy Spirit is at work. A miracle is God's way of inviting you to know Him personally—He communicates with us and reveals His character through His interventions. Miracles usually cause a reorienting of our lives so that we are more aligned with what the Holy Spirit has planned for us.

In miracles with an obvious supernatural touch by God, His magnificence is shown, but the people involved may not change. For example, the Israelites saw lots of these large one-way interventions like the plagues that got them released from Egypt, the parting the Red Sea, miraculous manna for food, and water from a dry rock. Yet, these things apparently did not reach or change their hearts with a few notable exceptions (Joshua and Caleb). In the personal, true stories in this current work, each principal character had a change in their heart and life. Perhaps that is because these were not easy, stand-by-and-watch miracles, but rather they were participatory. These miracles involved prayer, trust, and walking forward in faith. This book is about interventions by God that leave us changed in heart and actions.

Newton's first law of motion declares that "An object at rest stays at rest and an object in motion stays in motion with the same speed and in the same direction unless acted upon by an unbalanced force." In other words, things 'keep on doing what they're doing' unless something changes that. This physical law has a similar counterpart in our minds and spirits. We will keep thinking what we always thought, speaking like we always spoke, and acting the way we always acted unless something happens to change that. In other words, physical laws have their likenesses in the spiritual realm.

This is not to say that all change is good. Adam, our first ancestor, invited an enemy into our midst, so there are bad forces upon earth as well as God's hand at work. Yet, those who love God will label both the good and bad in our lives as 'Divine Providence'. In the big picture, God is always ultimately in control. Divine Providence means there are no coincidences (as well as no failures on God's part). God will always be the victor in the end, and for those who love God and are called according to his purpose, things will always work out for good.₁ This is a key point relating to miraculous events, because sometimes what looks bad from our viewpoint can bring about positive changes and eternal good (which, in my opinion, is an intrinsic part of true miracles).

The most obvious positive change of direction is when we choose to come into the kingdom of Christ. A true salvation experience is always a miracle because it involves a total alteration of course--a heart and action modification that we could never accomplish by our own effort. A one-eighty degree turn of direction that perseveres does not come about simply by trying to be good, by our human effort alone. It is supernatural. Using our natural human strength and resolutions, we will revert to old habits every time. These habits are our tendency to always keep on the same path with what we always thought, said, and did.

Redemption stories are wonderful and could fill this book, but I am going to share a variety of miracles to show a little part of how God works all around us. We can perceive what He is doing if we ask for the gift of eyes to see and ears to hear.[2] God only asks that we seek to know Him with all our heart.[3] We will not be able to fully perceive miracles in our lives if we do not allow the saving work of Christ to make us new creatures. That must be the starting point for true and lasting transformation.

Having our spiritual senses opened paves the way for grateful and hopeful hearts. In the Bible, when things got tough, the great heroes of the Bible would remember, recount, or rehearse the miracles that God did in the past.[4] That made them ready for what God was doing in the present and for the things that He would accomplish in the future.

You may be asking about the times when we ask for God's help, and He does not seem to show up. Confusing and hurtful, right? Just like anyone else, I have struggles with what feels like unanswered prayer. Related to this, my personal discovery is that for God-lovers, He is always there.[5] Period. No matter what. Even when we are at our lowest point, even when horrific things happen, even when we cannot feel his presence, He stays right with us. We may not be delivered from our situation, pain, or suffering, but we don't have to be alone. His name, Immanuel, (another name for Jesus, our Messiah) means 'God with us'. That is the very message on every page of the Bible. He is with us. That is huge.

Even more than that, for the period that we are here on the earth, God's presence is around all of us, Christians, and non-Christians alike. The Bible says that in Him we live and move and have our being.₆ This is not referring just to those committed to Christ. God's light, love, and mercy are present in this place (albeit sometimes in a murky way due to the presence of evil ₇). At the end of our lives, we can spend eternity in a place completely permeated by God, or we can choose to be separated from him forever in a place of total darkness where we are devoid even of self. In that void, we will continue for eternity, but our personhood and identity will no longer exist because that is linked with God whom we rejected.

I have no answers for why God says yes to some prayers and no to others, or to why terrible things happen in this world. Yet, this I know in complete surety—God is forever good. My life is built upon that truth! He always cares. He is involved with us in the here and now in this world (and forever if we make the choice to allow him to be Lord and Savior).₈ One thing I comprehend without doubt, none of us is good enough to deserve God's mercy and intervention— nonetheless, God chooses to generously pour out His love.

As I see it, there are different types of miracles. Coming to know God as Savior and Lord (Salvation), Protection, Healing, Provision, Miraculous Non-Coincidences, Encouragement, God's Gifts, God's Comfort, and Growing in Character (Sanctification). As much as possible, I will divide the book in that way, however, some stories fit in more than one category. Because I am organizing it in this manner, it will not always be in chronological order.

Moreover, I will share how these miracle stories have affected me personally. (It has been surprising how each story left an imprint on me, both in my perceptions and actions.) So that these are not just entertaining tales, I will ask some questions and make some observations to make us think and apply these stories in our lives.

This book is meant to help you to open your eyes and see the miracles, big and little, all around you. It is meant to build your faith and to give you hope. God is still speaking. He spoke the universe into existence and maintains it with a word. 9 He wants to speak to us in many ways--God has always talked to human beings since the time of Adam and Eve. Each time he communicates with us and helps us to change our trajectories to line up with his heart, it is a miracle. He is the creator, and we are the creatures, yet we are beloved and dear to him. We may be creatures, but we can become adopted sons and daughters of God if we accept his gift of reconciliation.

Once again, I say, God may not remove us from pain and suffering, but He has promised that He will always be with us. Stop, look, and listen for His presence. There is no miracle too small to be obvious to those who choose to let God help them see and hear. There is no miracle large enough to show up for those who prefer to remain blind and deaf so they cannot see and hear God at work. Say a prayer for open eyes, ears, and hearts before you start this journey! Enjoy these stories of God's interventions and faithfulness in ways as small as a whisper and as large as a shout.

CHAPTER 1--MIRACLES OF SALVATION

We all long to be fully known and completely loved. As close as some humans may come to giving this unconditional love, they will always fall short. The only one who can love us in our totality, including the not-so lovely portions, is our heavenly Father. Just as each of us is unique, so our salvation stories are all one-of-a-kind. God does not give us a one-size-fits-all type of love. He lets us know of his caring in very personal ways.

On the other hand, there is no other Savior besides Jesus. There are many wise, kind people with good advice and help. However, only one Savior came down from His throne in heaven to be our way to God. He chose to be the one to let us be right with God by offering us His own righteousness. Without that, we cannot be in the presence of God or in heaven.

To understand the need for salvation, read the creation story in Genesis. Adam walked in the garden with God, not as an equal but as a beloved child. By Adam's choice to disobey, the tendency to rebel entered the human heart. We are all natural mutineers against God and cannot defeat this inclination on our own. Jesus as part of the Godhead (Father, Son and Holy Spirit) has none of this predisposition towards rebellion, so He came to help us to restore our relationship with God. He chose to live as a man to conquer this bent towards evil that Adam introduced. He paid the price for all human beings--for the natural disobedience in our hearts. We must simply accept the gift of the sacrifice of His life on the cross and let Him be King of our lives. To understand this gift more fully, read C. S. Lewis's <u>Mere Christianity</u> or N. T. Wright's <u>Simply Christian</u>. Another great read is <u>The Case for Christ</u> by Lee Stroebel.

Christianity is the only religion (or attempted relationship) in which God reaches to us, instead of expecting us to pull ourselves up by our bootstraps and to earn our own way to Him. If you have ever tried to be perfect, then you already know that making our own way to God is impossible.

Soak in these salvation stories, each with its own fingerprint of God's love. We do not need to be alone-God is just waiting for an invitation into each of our lives

Meeting Jesus then Meeting Lee (McLaughlin family story)

During my junior and senior years in high school, I began the process of seriously trying to have a relationship with God. Having been in church my whole life, I had tried to read the Bible and pray. However, it felt like my prayers hit the ceiling and fell right back down, plus reading the Bible seemed like wading through a foreign language (for as much as I understood it).

In 1970, I was in my freshman year at West Virginia University, and I got the invitation to go to an Antioch weekend at Good Counsel Friary in Morgantown, West Virginia. Having no real idea what it meant, I agreed to go. The weekend took place during Thanksgiving break, and it consisted of teachings by lay people telling their stories of coming to know Jesus. Each presenter gave a part of the gospel message along with illustrations from their own lives. Even though I had gone to church my whole life and had likely heard this message many times, this was the first time my spiritual eyes and ears were opened to see and hear. It was literally like someone finally turned on a floodlight for me! As a result, I asked Jesus to be my Savior and for the Holy Spirit to live in me and be my guide. For the first time, I truly understood why Jesus died on the cross for my sins, and I gave the Lordship of my life over to God-- the Father, Son and Holy Spirit. I was infused with His love and with a whole different perspective on living.

During my first semester at West Virginia University, I had been dating Jim (not his real name). Jim and I quickly became quite serious and even committed to get married at some time in the nebulous future. (Looking back, it is easy to see that we were mismatched.) In my second semester at WVU, a momentous occasion happened--Jim introduced me to Lee McLaughlin, who was in our biology class.

The moment that I met Lee still sticks in my mind. I was struck by his good looks—he was a football player with a tall, muscular, and striking physique. However, what happened in that moment was more than just being taken by Lee's physical attractiveness—it was somehow a jolt of spirit-to-spirit connection. Strangely, that night I dreamed of marrying Lee McLaughlin. That was the very first of my dreams from God. As a new Christian, there was no basis for my understanding such things. Yet, even in my ignorance, I knew my dream was significant. Because I recognized it as a communication from God, I tucked the dream away in my heart.

Jim and I later broke up, and Lee very gradually guided what had been a friendship (during my time of being with Jim) to a full-fledged dating relationship. Next to the gift of connection with Himself as my heavenly Father, Son, and Holy Spirit, Lee has been my greatest treasure from God.

We have had such adventures together. Our marriage took place on Lee's twenty-first birthday while I was still twenty years old. As we each had much more maturing to do, we finished our growing up together. Both of us had (and still have) flaws and sins that have made life a challenge, but even cooperatively learning and stretching ourselves in these demanding things has been exciting.

In my opinion, there has never been a more steadfast, persevering, humble, kind, and resourceful man—he is my hero. He has learned to become more dependent on God during the time I have known him. Together, we have grown to trust God more and more as we have shared a lifetime of experiences, both good and bad.

Lee's name means "from the meadow". When Lee sweeps into your life, it is like a fresh breeze blowing in from the meadow, bringing hope, clean air, and the smell of sunshine.

Psalm 37:4 "Take delight in the LORD, and He will give you the desires of your heart."

Thank You, Lord, for drawing me to know you and for giving me a life lived in concert with you through the Holy Spirit. You were my greatest gift ever. Thanks, also, for the present of Lee. I didn't even know that Lee was a desire of my heart, but You knew, Father. Thank You, Father God, for my precious and faithful husband.
In Jesus' name, Amen

The Hound of Heaven

Many years ago, I met Mitch and Judy Santlofer at a business function. (My husband, Lee, had some business interactions with Mitch before that.) The four of us had dinner together, and Lee and I loved this couple right from the start. Mitch and Judy are not into small talk—they love to speak about things that matter. When we met them, Judy was a devoted Catholic, and Mitch was a non-devoted Jewish man. He was bar-mitzvahed to please his grandparents but had almost never stepped foot inside a temple.

Lee and I were struck by how respectful Mitch and Judy were to each other, even though they were on such different pages in their worldviews and belief systems. They made a close marriage by their very deliberate acts of kindness and gentle words towards each other.

Little did we know that during that business trip, we would be the first ones used by the Holy Spirit to get Mitch's spiritual eyes and ears attuned to what the Hound of Heaven had to show him.

During our dinner conversation, we talked about God, and I asked Mitch this question, "What is it like not to have Jesus in your life?" Mitch basically told me that Jesus had never been in his life and meant nothing to him. Later, Lee and I asked if he would read a book if I sent it. He said that he would at least give it a try. We sent him Lee Stroebel's book, The Case for Christ, which is a great book for looking into Jesus, who He is, and what He did (from a very factual investigative-reporter methodology). Mitch read the book, and the seeds were planted.

Let me catch you up on Mitch and Judy's back story. They married in 1977 and, despite their different faiths, were a good match. Judy was what is sometimes referred to as a 'cradle Catholic', meaning she went to church on Sundays and Holy Days, but Jesus was not a huge part of her life.

Twenty years into their marriage, Judy found her own deep faith in Christ. She came to personally understand having Jesus in her life—she also became quite involved in the church. Her life changed radically as she put God as priority number one. This did not sit well with Mitch and the kids, so Judy started seeing a counselor.

Following a few sessions, Mitch was invited to attend with her, then later he continued by himself. The counselor basically said that Judy had a right to her passionate faith if she did not neglect her family, and Mitch and their children needed to be respectful of Judy's life with God. The whole family found a way to make this work, and they became a model household in honoring each other.

A few months after we met Mitch and Judy for the first time at the business function, they got together with their friends-- Pete and Linda. Linda asked the same question almost word for word that I had asked Mitch, "What is it like to live without Jesus in your life?"

Mitch told his friends the same thing he had told me, "It does not matter. Jesus has never been a part of my life, and He means nothing to me." However, Linda, the friend who asked the question, gave him a challenge along with what is called the miraculous medal. She asked Mitch to say the Novena (a Catholic prayer) for nine days and see if it brought him any comfort. Mitch was always up for an investigative experiment, so he tried it. He found that the prayer did bring him comfort, and, therefore, he has been saying it every day since.

Judy never pushed her faith on Mitch, but that didn't mean she did not quietly leave books around for Mitch to 'happen' upon. Mitch secretly read these books, without saying anything to his wife--there was a pride issue for Mitch at this point.

Another time on a random Saturday morning, the television was on in the background, and Mitch's heart was grabbed by a commercial about Jesus as Lord and Savior. The Hound of Heaven was in hot pursuit of Mitch Santlofer, and he could not get Jesus out of his head. On this hallmark day, Mitch took Toby, their golden retriever, for a walk in their neighborhood. Mitch talked to Toby like a friend as they ambled along the sidewalk. On their way home Mitch noticed something glistening out in the middle of the street. "It is probably glass," he told Toby as he went to get it like a good citizen. To his utter shock, it was a solid gold crucifix on a chain laid out like a jewelry store display—it was oriented to show its best angle in exactly the direction Mitch was walking towards it.

At first Mitch just stood there in total astonishment saying out loud to his dog, "This is nuts!" Finally picking it up, Mitch moved to the side of the street, holding the necklace out like someone would come along and claim it, which no one did. He told Judy about it when he got home then called the church (which was nearby) in case someone reported it missing. Nobody stepped forward to say they lost it.

Mitch hung the crucifix in his armoire, and, unknown to Judy, he touched and admired it daily. (The crucifix later became a reminder of how God pursued him, and he now wears it around his neck every single day to remember God's great love.)

Mitch began thinking even more about this man Jesus--he even went to the library and began researching Him. He tried to find out all he could about Christianity, its history, and all the major players.

Meanwhile Judy had another concern. She approached

Mitch and asked him to check out the lump in her breast. Within a few days, an older woman at the church, out of the blue, 'happened' to talk to Judy about previously having breast cancer, which had since been healed. This was the impetus that Judy needed to propel her to see her doctor, who scheduled Judy's biopsy.

Later, the doctor called with the results at a time when Judy was not there, and he told Mitch the biopsy was cancerous. Mitch found Judy, told her the bad news, and they cried together for a bit. Then, Judy hopped up and said, "I have to go to church and find the priests!"

At the church, Father Sebastian was bustling around, but Judy approached him and said, "I need to talk to you." He dropped everything and talked to Judy and Mitch for an hour. The next day he said a special Mass just for Judy- Mitch was there in support of his wife. He had never knelt to pray in his life, but at one moment in the service, Mitch felt like he was thrown to his knees to pray. "Jesus you are calling me," was Mitch's prayer. The shove to his knees to pray was like getting a blow from a two-by-four to the head that brought him to wakefulness, then he had sudden insight that Jesus was using Judy's breast cancer to finally get Mitch's full attention. It was the last push to answer the call from the Hound of Heaven.

The next day, Judy came into the room where Mitch was ironing one of his shirts. She asked him what was going on. He said, "For the last twenty-three years, I never went to church with you, but for the next twenty-three, I will never miss a Sunday." In his heart, Mitch decided to check out Catholicism for his chosen denomination.

This decision was confirmed when a mass-mailing was sent by Judy's parish. Typically, these mailings were addressed to Mr. and Mrs. Mitch Santlofer. The letter that Mitch received was addressed just to Mitch Santlofer, which he opened and read with avid interest. (Judy saw the letter first but carefully resealed it and kept quiet. Just like she did when leaving books around for Mitch to 'happen upon', she never said a word about seeing the letter.)

Judy later thanked the priest for sending a special letter out to Mitch about the Rite for Christian Initiation for Adults (RCIA) which gave instruction on how adults could convert to Catholicism. Father Michael said that there was no special letter sent to Mitch. The RCIA letters went out in a mass-mailing, and somehow "Mr. and Mrs." was left off. The letter was addressed just to Mitch, and he took it as a personal letter from God.

Today, you can ask Mitch any question about his church. He knows what everything symbolizes, the deeper meaning of teachings, and the history behind them. Mitch now leads classes for Confirmation to kids in the church. There could not be a better teacher—Mitch not only has head-knowledge; he also has heart-commitment. These kids will be taught what it means to know Jesus as their Lord and Savior, and they will see it in action in Mitch's life. Mitch was informed that his Sacraments of Baptism, First Holy Communion, and Confirmation would be administered at the Easter Vigil. Judy and Mitch were both in awe to see that the date was April 14, 2001. April 14 is Mitch's birthday, and it was a final love-pat from God to let Mitch know how very cherished he is by his heavenly Father.

Luke 19:10 "For the Son of Man came to seek and to save the lost."

Matthew 18:12 "What do you think? If a man has a hundred sheep, and one of them has gone astray, does he not leave the ninety-nine on the mountains and go in search of the one that went astray?"

Thank You, Lord, that you pursue each of us. You do everything to get our attention. You are the Hound of Heaven, and You love us so much. In Jesus' name, Amen

More Than We Can Ask or Imagine

Gail and I became fast friends in 1998 through a prayer group for our kids, and we immediately connected at a deep level. Without knowing me for long, Gail invited me to be part of a mission trip to Mexico. That started our adventures together, and we have been fast friends and soul-buddies ever since. We understand each other in a way that is rare. Gail was my first 'forever friend'—I have absolutely no doubt that we will also be best friends for all eternity.

Let me tell you a little about Gail--she is a loyal friend who sticks closer than a brother[10] (or sister). She cheerfully helps anytime she sees a need. No matter how far apart we live from each other, she puts out the effort to make sure we stay well-connected. Gail is not superficial—she invests in the deeper and more eternal parts of life, while always keeping her sense of fun. Gail is a phenomenal dancer who won a major contest for line dancing. She is well educated and pretty, but she never looks down on anyone. With the rare gift of seeing the strengths in others, Gail is one of those people whom I call a 'connector'. She draws people towards each other and nearer to God, as she encourages individuals to become their best selves in Christ. Gail and I were at a conference, and I was on stage as a volunteer subject to allow the leaders to demonstrate prayer counseling. Immediately after the session was over (as I was coming down from the stage), a stranger came up to Gail and asked her if we were friends. He said that the Lord showed him a golden cord connecting the two of us— our hearts were linked with a glowing gold bond.

The time in Gail's life that I met her was at the end of the chain of events in this story--I did not know Gail when she was at her lowest point (depressed, beaten down, and without hope). The Gail that I have always known is filled with joy and peace; she is a leader of women; and she has a bounce in her walk as well as a smile in her eyes. When Gail and I went on our Mexico mission trip, all the high school girls would gather around her like bees to honey. They copied her because she is attractive in soul and spirit—I have always imitated her also. Of course, Gail never even saw any of that, because of her totally humble attitude.

After the Mexico mission trip, Gail and I led years of classes together to help broken women (like us) through an in-depth Biblical program called Elijah House, "an inner healing ministry that equips and empowers individual hearts to be healed and changed"[11].

Gail's uncrushable spirit, positive attitude, and peace in every circumstance changed people around her because they could see Jesus in her. People approach Gail for advice because she has soaked the Bible up so much that it comes out her pores—she is intelligent but also wise. Gail is my beautiful friend, and I thank God for her in my life.

This story is about a life filled with miracles, beginning with getting to know God, the biggest miracle of all. God intervenes in our lives for the goal of bringing us into relationship with Him, also to guide us into His purposes for us, and to preserve us to be able to accomplish those plans. He also simply loves to give us the desires of our hearts![12] As you read this story, note how God gave Gail her wildest heart-dreams--more than she could even ask or imagine.[13] Here is the tale recounted in Gail's words.

"I grew up in the church, attended Catholic school, and had loving parents. My first three years were spent mainly in the company of my grandparents in their home on the south side of Chicago. My parents, older brother, and I lived in my grandparents' garage. Both Mom and Dad worked to try to afford a home of our own therefore were not around very much. Grandma Clara often babysat for four toddlers: my brother (John), my two cousins (Tom and Terry), and me. Grandma was almost completely blind, and Grandpa was not usually at home to help her. As the youngest and the only girl, I was relegated to a playpen much of the time. (Later, a prophet told me of a vision that he had of me crying and crying in a playpen with no rescue in sight.) This was the point in my life that a deep shadow settled upon me."

"From that time on, I had periods of depression. I was quiet and shy, rarely speaking. Until the age of six, I spoke my own version of 'baby speak', with my brother functioning as my interpreter. School was always a struggle—only recently (at the age of 68) did I discover that I have a learning disability that affects one per cent of the population. It is called aphantasia. This is a condition in which I cannot picture things in my brain. It explains why I had difficulty learning things in school, as well as many of my other struggles in life."

"As a middle school student in the 1950's, I had gender dysphoria (sexual confusion), and at thirteen years old, I approached my mom to request a sex change operation, which I am so grateful that my mother refused. I began dating boys at sixteen but struggled with bulimia until I was thirty-one. Now, I realize that I saw only deficits in myself and let them define me. To my horror, this negative focus brought about a rejection and self-hatred that reared its ugly head in the days, months, and years to follow."

"I would describe my life at that time as joyless. Quiet and shy, I hardly spoke at all. My views of myself told me that I was worthless and lower than everyone else—I was extremely depressed. Thoughts of suicide plagued me, and I was a master at casting blame on myself and everyone around me."

"Vatican II came out of the Catholic church in my junior year in high school. I was aghast that I had to remove my tiny statue of Saint Christopher from my push button '60's Plymouth Valiant dashboard. The church now declared Saint Christopher to be only a myth. The rules, from my teenage perspective, had whimsically been changed. Prior to Vatican II, a person could eat a hot dog on Friday that could ultimately send them to hell if not confessed--it was a sin. However, with the changes from Vatican II, the church lifted the ruling and determined that one could now enjoy a slab of meat on Fridays without any repercussions. It was no longer a sin that merited punishment. My gut feeling was that God's commands should never change— if they do then this must all be man's invention. I honestly felt that changing rules was disingenuous, and therefore I rejected the Church. I moved into a whole new set of laws—'do whatever you want, as long as you don't hurt anyone'."

"I became a hippie flowerchild of the 1960's and 1970's. Picture straight long, blond hair with bangs, bell-bottoms, and all the attitudes that typically went along with that. I became a partygoer and the car-driver for my group of friends. On weekends, I did a lot of drinking and other things of which I am not proud."

"Although I had been working at jobs since I was fifteen years old, I could not find direction, switching from major to major in college. During my university experience, I had my second serious bout with depression—I fantasized about escaping with a jump from the highest building on campus. Little did I realize at the time that God was about to rescue me again."

"While attending a campus dance in quite a loopy state (from drinking), I met a tall, handsome, and somewhat forward student who asked me to dance. My future hubby won me over when he handed me a stick of gum and said, "You need this." Jim happened to be a senior, graduating with a degree in biology, which was also my current major. He advised me to switch to medical technology, which I did. (His advice was good--I worked happily at a local hospital for twenty-eight years upon my graduation.) And yes, I have been married to that good-looking, bold man for forty-nine years.

"Unhappy with myself and needing a scapegoat, the darkness that entered me as a baby in the playpen began to dominate my life once again. This heaviness enveloped my thoughts, and I was soon contemplating divorce. My feelings consumed me. To be able to live with myself, I placed the blame on Jim and concluded that I had married the wrong guy. Once again, I found life to be joyless, and I wanted out of married life."

"My two sons were now six and four, and I was pregnant again with Brett, my 'bonus baby'. (Jim and I had agreed that we could comfortably afford only two children, but God knew better than we did.) Yet, my plans for leaving my husband were about to be foiled by another 'God intervention', unbeknownst to me."

"When I needed a shoulder to cry on, my grade school friend, Rosie, came to my rescue. However, she seemed different, somehow changed, and transformed. I wanted her to console me and to agree with my intentions to leave Jim. Instead, she kept saying the solution to my problems was to have a relationship with Jesus. This left me feeling betrayed and like she was forcing this Jesus-person down my throat. Yet, there was something about Rosie that was remarkably different--she had a special joy about her (She was always smiling and cheerful amidst a tough life.) She was sure that Jesus, her new-found friend, and savior, could help me also."

"Rosie succeeded in convincing me to give this Jesus a try-- I was totally desperate. Every time I looked at Rosie's face, I saw joy! That's what I had desired for all my life--I craved what she had! Whatever it was that had transformed my best friend into a hopeful, contented wife and mom--I wanted it. So, I talked to Rosie's Jesus as if He was with us in the living room. This Jesus is God who loves me and died for my sins so that I could be loved by Him, know Him, and call Him my friend."

"I asked Jesus to forgive me for my sins (even though at the time I thought I wasn't a sinner). Additionally, I asked him to take control of my life--this was something I knew that I needed and wanted because my life was a train wreck. For me, this moment was the actual start of my real living--the miracle of miracles! The events that followed in the years ahead were bespattered with meetings with Jesus through prayer, God-rescues, and miracles."

"In spite of my new friendship with God, feelings of depression and worthlessness still weighed me down, nonetheless, I had the beginnings of joy that increased each time I received an answer from Him. He showed His reality and love to me as He daily involved Himself in my life in response to my prayers. Since then, I have experienced countless miracles—more than imaginable.

My first Bible study was on Philippians, and my heart's cry became then and still is, "I want to run the race to reach the prize which is a life in Christ."₁₄. I have also truly discovered that God's 'steadfast love is better than life' and he 'blesses us as long as we live'₁₅."

God began to give Gail more than she could ask or imagine. She began a new relationship with the Lord by starting out every morning with the prayer, "Jesus, you have to be real!" Her friend, Rosie, told her to read the Bible, but the Bible made no sense to her. Rosie's answer to this was, "Find a Bible study." Gail called every church in town, but all Bible studies were too far along for her to join them.

Our God provides in His own mysterious ways! When Gail took Brett, her infant son, to swim lessons at a local pool, a stranger sat next to her as they waited on the kids' lessons. This lady invited Gail to a Bible study in her home—just three blocks from Gail's house. Gail went and was amazed by these women who talked about Jesus like they knew Him personally.

At this point, Gail still desired a divorce. She decided to ask God about it. She did the thing where you open the Bible and point to a Bible verse. Here is the scripture she read: 'For I hate divorce!" says the Lord, the God of Israel'.₁₆ (Gail does not recommend doing this method of hearing from God. It is not really the best way to get messages from the Lord, but as a new believer it was the best she could do.)

In addition to this new knowledge about how God feels about divorce, Gail's aunt (a Christian woman whom Gail rarely saw and who knew nothing at all about Gail's life) sent her a book out of the blue. This book was titled <u>Love Life for Every Married Couple</u> by Ed Wheat. (Gail later found out that this book was used for marriage conferences and retreats for healing and strengthening marriages.) In one chapter, Dr. Wheat addressed the spouse who no longer feels any love. He gave scriptures plus actions to restore that emotion.

At that stage in her walk with Christ, Gail told Jim that she might be acting differently because she was a Christian now. She began to do the steps that Ed Wheat gave in the book. Some were simple, like greeting your spouse at the door with a smile, kiss, and encouraging word. Others were more challenging, like never saying no to your husband's sexual overtures. Both Gail and her friend Rosie had already learned not to say a detrimental word about your spouse.

Miraculously, Gail began to see changes in Jim. Now, as she reflects on that period, Gail says it was really she who changed.

Gail put her kids in Christian school (another miracle, in that Jim agreed to this) and sought out churches filled with the Holy Spirit and sound teaching. She became involved in worship and her eyes were opened to God's touch all around her. Here is her statement about miracles: "The only way you can know Jesus personally is that he does miracles which He designs exactly for you."

Meanwhile, Gail's son, Ryan responded to her prayers and influence, plus the good teaching and love of a godly Sunday school teacher. He committed his life to Christ at ten years old. Ryan is a quiet but dynamic Christian who makes large ripples of influence with his life. He later got his Master of Divinity degree and became a 'shepherd of men' then moved to a more impactful role in a major publishing company. Ryan was the first in the far reaching effects of Gail's life-change.

Soon after that, Todd became a believer as a very young child. He also was influenced by his mom and the same loving Sunday school teacher. Todd now serves as a volunteer in a mission to the homeless, in addition to his day job.

For a period after that, Gail went through a drifting time in her life. God got kicked out of top priority, and she filled her time with lots of other activities. As a result of this, Gail's and Jim's marriage reached an all-time low. They tried counseling, which made their relationship worse. Finally, Jim knew their marriage was on its dying breath.

In addition to his home life, Jim was having problems in the workplace—his whole life was crumbling. Knowing he was about to lose his family, he approached Gail in June of 1998. He said, "Marriage counseling is not working. I need God's help. How do I become a Christian?"

Gail led him through prayer that was something like this, "Jesus, I recognize that you died for me on the cross—I have sinned against you and lived in a manner not pleasing to you. Please forgive me, I got it all wrong. I need you in my life. I need your Holy Spirit to live in me and take control of my life." Jim rocketed into the Christian life, devouring the Bible, and soaking up teaching like a sponge. Within a year, he was leading other men in Bible studies. This gentle-hearted man began investing not only in God but also in his wife and his son Brett, who was the only son left at home. Gail and Brett were both deeply affected by his nurturing and love. Gail at long last felt the emotion that she had longed for in her marriage.

Brett said he never saw anyone change so quickly and totally as his dad. Brett became the last one in the household to come into the Kingdom of God after seeing God's amazing work in his own father. Brett is now a

pastor in Korea. He has a servant's heart and is a great
evangelist.

The ripple effects of Gail's rich life with Christ keep
occurring as her love for Jesus spreads throughout the
world and to new generations through all of those she has
influenced. Gail has had huge effects on me personally.

To finish this story, here is a quote from Gail, "I have
discovered through knowing Christ that all people matter to
Him. Scars become blessings and the pathways to meeting
Jesus. When calling on Him through prayer becomes the
answer to life's problems, then you will find your joy. "

To Gail's words I say, "Amen!" Here is to all of us broken
people—may we bring other shattered people to Jesus, who
is the only answer to our crushed spirits, souls, and bodies.
(By the way, if you think you are perfect, then you are the
most broken of all!)

Ephesians 3:20. "Now to him who is able to do
immeasurably more than all we ask or imagine, according
to his power that is at work within us"

Thank You, Lord, for Your response to the things we pray.
You give us even more than we can ask or imagine. Thanks
for caring about the desires of our hearts and for giving us
what we truly need. In Jesus' name, Amen

The Scarlet Thread

The exact time that I learned about the scarlet thread eludes
me, but since then it has been a fascination for me. It is a
subject that Bible scholars have discussed, and they will
say different things about the meanings of scarlet thread
references in scripture (there are quite a few).[17]

Here is what it means to me in very simple terms: the
scarlet thread represents God's constant presence in our

lives--our pathway to freedom. (Freedom from wounds, shame, guilt, and the consequences of sinful choices that oftentimes result in a prison of our own making.) This beautiful thread not only keeps us from eternal separation from God, but it is the only Way to lasting healing and peace. The scarlet thread allows us to experience God's presence throughout our lifetimes spent here on earth. You may wonder how we cooperate with God to let Him weave Himself into our lives as our scarlet thread.

This story of an event is a miracle highlighting what only the Master could conceive. It is a real-life example of how to unite with and give God, the ultimate artist, permission to weave the scarlet thread into our lives. When we ask for and receive this glorious gift of reconciliation with God, the Master Artist creates a beautiful tapestry that brings eternal purpose and beauty that is unsurpassed.

The scarlet thread represents Christ's work on the cross through the shedding of his blood which thereby saves us from going our own sinful way into destruction and loss of perpetuity with God. This thread is more than just what keeps us from eternal separation from God, it is what weaves through our lives to make them everlastingly significant and beautiful. You may wonder how we cooperate with God to let him weave himself into our lives so that our time here is not just wasted breath.

This story is a real-life example of how to unite with God to allow the scarlet thread to become interlaced into our lives and beings until we become part of a beautiful tapestry that will bring eternal meaning and splendor that we cannot imagine. This tale is about my friend, Gail (who cringes each time I hold her up as an illustration yet submits to being an example if it will help someone else).

Gail did not commit her life to serving and loving God until her third decade. She had no real idea how to do life with God but decided to say yes to anything that God had for her. This meant lots of adventures but also terrifying feelings of ineptitude as Gail moved into each new assignment with trepidation. (To give you an idea of how incompetent we both felt, before any assigned task, we would get there early and pray together like crazy for the Holy Spirit to help us. It is also telling that for both of us, our favorite song is 'Jesus Loves Me', because in every step forward we relied on His love and presence to get us through.)

A shared assignment that we each felt called to do was prison ministry. Both of us started this in our fourth decade, and neither of us had any clue whatsoever how to do it. Initially, a friend named Bruce told us about a ministry near us in a youth detention center--he said that we would be trained in how to do ministry when we went to the Illinois Youth Center in St. Charles, Illinois. This is a two-level mid-security detention center—at the time we went, it housed thirteen to seventeen-year-old boys who had done serious crimes.

It was a gorgeous, sunny Saturday when we went to the St. Charles prison for the organized event that would train us in how to minister to incarcerated youth, which took place outside on the lovely grounds of the Youth Center. Our training session was short and sweet, not at all what we were expecting. We were each given a small, thin booklet with simple diagrams, scriptures, and the gospel message in easy-to-understand terms. We were simply to read this aloud to our group, ask for any questions, then ask if any wanted to pray the sinner's prayer with us (this simply means telling God we are sorry about our old lives and are ready to commit to serving Christ). That was the full extent of our training—to say we felt unprepared was an understatement.

The event was very well organized. It started with some demonstrations of remarkably well-trained dogs who went to unbelievable lengths of obedience to please their masters. Next, a body builder showed crazy feats of strength. Finally, former prison inmates gave stories of their changed lives with Jesus. Each story or demonstration pointed to Christ and showed how to let Him be the Master of your life. The stories were beyond amazing, and the boy-inmates watched with rapt attention.

With our hearts beating fast in apprehension, the newly trained (would-be or maybe wannabe) evangelists then took a small group of boys. Gail's group included six or seven boys who all listened politely as she went through her booklet. This was her first time telling the whole gospel message like this. At the end of going through the booklet, she asked the boys if anyone wanted to pray with her. The response was deafening silence. After a moment, she asked if any of the young men just wanted to chat with her. A lad named Chris spoke up, and the rest of the group moved away leaving Gail and Chris alone to talk.

Gail later related to me, "I was uncertain on how to proceed--this turn of events was left out of the manual. Chris was friendly and seemed eager to have a conversation, so I ventured to inquire about his family, siblings, his mom, and his dad. He became animated at once, asking if he could get his photo book of his family. As he left, I spoke to my Lord, 'What next?' Chris came back and shared photos of his mom, his grandpa, and others--his relatives were almost all in prison. His father was not in the scrapbook at all because he was never part of Chris's life (this seemed to be the case with so many of the incarcerated youth); his mom had stabbed someone to death in a bar fight; and the scrapbook pictures of his relatives all had equally sad stories (mostly involving murder). I was unnerved by what I heard but tried to stay calm and natural. Every family member was incarcerated, except one. (He mentioned that his stepdad was a Christian who was not in prison.) Shaken deeply, I was reeling from shock! This sweet youth reminded me of my own three sons, and he seemed very innocent and likeable. He loved his family regardless of their actions."

"And then it happened! The scarlet thread had been offered and accepted! Chris suddenly switched topics and asked me if he could say the prayer to have fellowship with Jesus!"

Gail led him through a prayer in which he asked for forgiveness for living his life in ways that were not lined up with God's way (repentance of sin). He asked for the gift of eternal life with God and for the Holy Spirit to take control of directing him. Chris gave Gail a photo of himself towering over his stepdad (the one whom he had casually mentioned was a Christian).

He wanted to keep in touch with Gail, so Gail arranged to have him send letters to her church and she wrote back in care of the prison. Gail urged Chris to get into a Bible study, and Chris started on a new trajectory in life. (Gail and he kept in touch for a few years.)

A bell rang at the end of the allotted time for this session, and Gail went to rejoin her group. While she did this, she noticed the young men pointing at her and whispering among themselves. Finally, someone came up to her and explained the buzz.

"The young man you were talking to—do you know who he is?" Of course, Gail did not know anything about him.

"He is a Satan worshipper. All the young men here are terrified of him because he has powers. He can make bad things happen, so they all stay away from him."

Gail was amazed--to her, this blond-haired, blue-eyed, cute-as-could-be boy was like one of her sons. She had an instant love for him when they talked. She could never have imagined him doing mean things to people or serving an evil master.

Nonetheless, God is no respecter of persons, and this boy chose to open his heart to the Holy Spirit and change directions by one hundred and eighty degrees. What a miracle to change course so completely and dramatically!

Moreover, Gail's putting herself into God's path to be available for His use was equally miraculous. How did Gail become a vehicle to carry God's love and hope to people around her? Gail said miracles were necessary for that. These were God's way of communicating to her. "I needed these workings from God that were tailored to me to keep going. Serving God would not be possible for me without God, Himself, showing up." Gail also showed up for each assignment and trusted God to be there with her—she has become a gorgeous tapestry exhibiting God's love.

Her heart's desire is that everyone would have the joy of knowing God—she prays and lives to bring about revival. The verses below are about John the Baptist preaching repentance. It could also be Gail's life verse, seeking revival for us all. What is revival? It is a spiritual awakening from a state of dormancy or ignorance. It includes finding a love for God, an understanding of His holiness, a passion for the Bible and Christ's church, a convicting agreement to our personal and corporate sin, a spirit of humility, and a desire to go in God's direction and grow in being right with Him.

Isaiah 40:3-5 "A voice cries out, "Listen! It's the voice of someone shouting, Clear the way through the wilderness for the Lord! Make a straight highway through the wasteland for our God! Fill in the valleys, and level the mountains and hills. Straighten the curves, and smooth out the rough places. Then the glory of the Lord will be revealed, and all people will see it together. The Lord has spoken!"

Father, we cannot do anything lasting or meaningful without You. Jesus, You are the scarlet thread who decorates our lives with purpose and love. Please weave Yourself into every fiber of our lives and create masterpieces from each of us. In Jesus' name, Amen

Abiding in the Vine

This story came from my long-term best friend, Gail. She has been the source of much wisdom in my life. From her, I have learned to look deeply into both the most simple and complex things to find where Christ is working.

Gail is devoted to her grandkids and pours herself into them, but always in ways that are cognizant of eternity. Here is a short and sweet story about Gail and her grandson Isaac.

This favorite song of Gail's starts off the tale: "In the moments where You go unnoticed, in the ordinary day to day, countless miracles of life around us point like arrows to Your name."[18]

Always watching for opportunities to build up the faith of those around her, and especially her grandkids, Gail sent an email to her oldest grandson, Isaac. She explained that her friend was writing a book on miracles, and she felt that Isaac coming to know the Lord and learning to live by the prompting of the Holy Spirit and by the Bible's teachings was a good fit for the book. She asked if she could interview him to get his story.

Isaac readily consented to the dialogue, and Gail was keeping her spiritual eyes and ears open to listen to promptings from the Holy Spirit during their weekend visit. The small nudge came as they were sitting in unseasonably cold weather watching Isaac's younger sister play a soccer game. Gail glanced behind her and saw thirteen-year-old Isaac sitting off by himself bundled up in his winter coat intently reading his novel. She heard the still, small voice of the Spirit prompting her to talk with him. This was the conversation:

Gail: "Isaac, why did you get baptized three years ago?"

Isaac: "I was a believer, so I just wanted everyone to know."

Gail: "Why do you believe in God?"

Isaac: "I want to go to heaven--I don't want to go to hell."

Gail: "Are you familiar with the parables Jesus shared with his listeners, especially the one about abiding in the vine? Jesus says if you abide in the vine (which represents Jesus), you will bear much fruit."

Isaac: "Yeah, if you don't bear fruit, the Gardener, God, will cut you off and throw you in the fire."

Gail: "So, what fruit do you see in your personal growth because you've been "abiding in the vine" for three years now?"

Isaac: "Well, I'm saying more "I'm sorry's." and "Thank you's." rather than "Please (I want this or that)."

Not wanting to impose on him further, Gail thanked him and returned to watching his sister's soccer game. It was a short interview, nevertheless it was filled with simple truth.

The next morning was Sunday, and as Gail and Isaac walked into the sanctuary, he grabbed her arm and whispered excitedly, "Look Grandma! The message is on "Abiding in the Vine!"

Gail gave a quick reply before they went to their seats, "God just gave you a little squeeze." While she said this, Gail affectionately squeezed his arm. (This little illustration may be a word picture that sticks with Isaac showing how involved God is in every detail of his life.)

Gail quotes the Bible, saying, "Whenever a person turns (in repentance and faith) to the Lord, the veil is taken away."[19] We behold His glory, and a miracle takes place-we become one of God's children. Before we become sons or daughters of God by giving our lives to Jesus, we have a veil in front of our spiritual eyes. We cannot perceive the things of God. Once we repent of going our own way, that veil is torn away. Then we can begin to see and participate in, 'Countless miracles around us in the ordinary day-to-day.'"

Gail will continue to add little treasures into the lives of those around her. When I think of my friend, I often think of this verse:

Proverbs 25:11. "A word fitly spoken is like apples of gold in a setting of silver."

Father, stories of coming to the kingdom show Your intervention in our lives. Our growing in character to more resemble Jesus is also certainly a miracle. Moreover, speaking words of life and hope at just the right time and in the right words is another small miracle. Please help us to hear You clearly and to speak fit words as led by the Holy Spirit. In Jesus' name, Amen

Conclusions

One could argue that miracles of salvation are the only ones that are eternal. A physically healed person will still get sick again and eventually die. Miracles of protection or provision fill a temporary need. A miracle may glorify God and echo that magnificence for eternity, but the only God-to-man interventions which last forever are changes to our hearts so that we belong to Him for eternity.

Each story of coming to know Jesus is markedly different, with God's voice and love coming in varied ways to each person. Just like each couple's 'falling in love' story is unique, so our beginning of a relationship with God is tailor-made.

Notice with my salvation story, I had a felt-need to know God at an early age. Mitch in 'The Hound of Heaven' story, Lee in his 'superman moment', and Gail in 'More than We Can Ask or Imagine' did not come to the realization of the void in their lives until circumstances piled up to take away their comfort. No matter the route that brings each of us into the kingdom, it is ultimately God who completes it. We cannot force ourselves into belonging to Christ without God's help—the Holy Spirit must be a part of that process.

Isaac's words about saying more apologies since becoming a Christian seem noteworthy (in the 'Abiding in the Vine' story). My own relationship with God seems closer when I am willing to repent more quickly and keep shorter accounts with God and others. When we commit to follow Jesus, we are heading towards True North. However, in the process of living, it seems so easy to deflect from the direct trajectory towards God. Constant readjustments are necessary in the form of repentance to stay on the correct compass setting.

Although they seem simple, Isaac's words about wanting to go to heaven and not to hell were also speaking for us all. We are drawn to Christ because of His love, but heaven is what we all desire for eternity. Missing out on life in God's presence would be the worst kind of hell.

My personal reaction to these stories is simple: I want to be responsive to the Holy Spirit so that I can say the right words at the perfect time to help draw people into God's realm. (Not too many words and not too few.) How many people were there for me at just the best time saying the exact words that I needed? (Or sometimes no words at all—merely hugs, tears, or simply being a loving presence.) Perhaps, even more importantly, I want to be a part of the petitioning process of praying people into the Kingdom. It is my strongly held belief that we are all brought into God's dominion, at least partly, through prayer (perhaps by someone we don't even know).

The events in each story show circumstances that bring each heart to the place of embracing God. Gail's friend, Rosie, exuded joy that Gail desperately needed. Mitch's wife, Judy, patiently waited with her mouth shut, quietly putting books or pamphlets around for Mitch to pick up as he was ready. In my life, a lover of God patiently answered my questions and guided me to a place where I could be taught. Some hoe the ground of a heart to soften up the soil; others plant seeds; some fertilize; and still others give 'Son-light' to help the plant break through. Often, I think the truly important thing is to just show up and trust that God will help, like Gail did in the prison ministry. No task is small in the light of the eternal consequences—the Sunday school teacher who faithfully taught and loved Gail's kids may have a whole group of people come to her heaven one day to say thank you for their life with the King of the Universe.

Questions to ponder:

1. Do you have a story to share about meeting Jesus for the first time? If not, have you asked Him to give you this (a definite beginning of your journey with Him)? Just like a commitment to our spouse needs a public declaration of joining together in marriage, so our relationship with God needs that defining point.
2. We all need to hear each other's stories. We should not be rushing through life so much that we cannot take time for this. Have your shared your story with others? If not, consider doing so without putting it off.

CHAPTER 2—MIRACLES OF PROTECTION

Did you ever look back at the details of a tough time and realize that you were protected? If that person had not been present, if it had happened with different timing, or in a different location; then the good outcome would not have been possible. God protects us! We just need to open our eyes to see it and cultivate an attitude of gratitude.

Growing in Humility and Dependence on God

Gradually, Bob was able to open his eyes. He had regained consciousness moments before, but his eyelids remained too heavy to open. Sounds began to penetrate his mind as he tried to orient himself. He heard small squeaking sounds and clicks which he started to recognize as bats flying around. It dawned on Bob that he was in a cave, then he perceived his friend, Bill, yelling to him that he had been hit by a rock. Bob's head was pounding with unbelievable pain as he sought to understand what had happened.

This life-changing story is about young Bob Ulfers. Through a series of miraculous events, Bob was pulled back from death's door and became a humble, Holy Spirit-dependent worker to the harvest of Jesus.

My impression of Bob Ulfers from my conversation with him is that he is a gentle man with a robust but subtle sense of humor. He comes across as transparent and humble. Bob wanted to know my motivation in writing this book, because his overwhelming desire is that this story gets out only for the end of glorifying God.

Bob is in a Bible study with my brother, who connected us for this book. Listening to Bob's chronicle brought me a fresh view of how caring and detailed our God is. The event which I recount here was a part of the preparation of Bob for the ministry into which he was called. Prepare to hear about miracle after miracle in this story.

Bob Ulfers was raised in the church, but until a year before this story took place, he viewed Christianity as little more than a set of traditions, rather than a Fatherchild relationship and way of living. About twelve months before this event happened, Bob had committed his life to loving and serving Jesus—this brought great changes in him. As a young Christian, Bob was just starting to dive into and enjoy studying scripture. He was even aiming towards doing Bible translation but had not reached the point of understanding his total dependence on God. Bob said that maybe there was some pride in his heart—possibly even the thought that God was "lucky to have him".

Bob had also become part of many campus' Christian organizations including Intervarsity Christian Fellowship and Fellowship of Christian Athletes. Christian community had grown to be a large part of his life.

Bob was an adventurous, outdoorsy, and nature-loving type of young man. He attended Virginia Tech, in Blacksburg, Virginia, when this tale began, so he had plenty of gorgeous environment to explore in the surrounding Appalachian Mountains. He was part of the Virginia Tech

Cave Club—a large number and rich variety of caves were present nearby for this group's adventures.

If you have never been to this area of the country, Virginia Polytechnical Institute (VPI), also known as Virginia Tech, is situated on a plateau between two majestic mountain ranges, the Allegheny, and the Blue Ridge Mountains. Transforming waters and time have softened the terrain but left many dramatic natural wonders that are breathtaking. This beautiful area is a favorite part of the world for many people for good reason.

Imagine the robust, vital, young Bob Ulfers setting about his life with enthusiasm and vigor in his university years. His idea of fun was to do challenging and extreme adventures. Bob loved life, loved God, and loved the evidence of God's hand all around him in the majesty of the New River Valley with the surrounding glorious, lush mountains. What an attractive picture of an independent and able young man. This man was gifted with a special blessing from God. However, Bob Ulfers was soon to discover and grow into a new humility and dependence upon his Lord.

On April 17, 1982, Bob was nineteen years old when he went on a caving trip with three others to experience his first vertical cave. This type of cave is created by underground waterfalls hollowing out pits with vertical walls. The cave that these young men set out to explore was Buddy Penley's Cave, a privately owned cavern in Bland County, Virginia.

The other three in the group were Pete, Mike, and Bill. Pete was the expert spelunker among the four young men. The other three had less experience with this type of cave—Bob was the only one in the group who had never done a vertical cave excursion.

The night before the climb, the group practiced repelling on a bridge. They diligently checked and rechecked all their ropes and equipment, and everything was going according to plan.

To picture general cave architecture, imagine big rooms or spaces with small entryways between them. Nonetheless, Buddy Penley's cave was more than a typically challenging structure in every way. To get an idea of what exploring this cavern was like, understand that one of the transitions between rooms was called "chest compressor". This cave gave every demand possible, from tight squeezes to high cliffs. Just to get to the vertical part of the experience was quite a physical feat.

Deep within the cave, the vertical portion began. Here a waterfall had dug a large pit—it created a sort of upside-down funnel, with the top being narrow and the bottom wide (about fifty feet across). The group free-rappelled to the bottom—it was one-hundred-twenty breath-stopping feet down. Free rappelling is a controlled descent on a rope in which the climber is not in contact with the rock. It is climbing without a belay (or attachment into the rock) except at the top. This is usually very high risk, and these climbers surely had to have a huge adrenaline rush. Thankfully, they safely reached and explored the bottom, and at this point, it was nearing 5:00 pm.

At the bottom of the pit, there was another active waterfall next to the large one-hundred- twenty-foot pit which was now dry. This smaller one still had water flowing and went another thirty feet down. The spelunkers avoided this area because of the wetness. In a short amount of time, they were done exploring and ready to go back up the one-hundred-twenty-foot vertical wall. Pete asked Mike to go up about ninety feet to a ledge to be a relay for the other climbers—he was to pass along instructions because it was hard to hear with the waterfall.

Through no fault of his own, Mike dislodged a large rock under the ledge, without even knowing it happened (therefore he could not call out a warning). The rock weighed about thirty pounds and dropped approximately ninety feet in a silent fall.

Bob and Pete were together below, with Pete giving some last-minute instruction for the climb to the top of the cliff.

Thankfully, Bob was looking down at the ropes and equipment on his shoulder instead of looking upward. If he had been looking up or even straight forward, it probably would have been instant death or at least a much worse injury. Pete had his hands on Bob's shoulders, so their injuries essentially happened as one unit. The large rock hit Bob's head, fracturing his skull and both sides of his fifth and sixth cervical vertebrae, then it slammed down on Pete, breaking both arms (one in five places). The rock ended up landing on Bob's foot causing another broken bone there.

Typically, a spine fracture such as Bob's would cause quadriplegia—that it did not was miraculous. Bob's skull was crushed inward by the boulder, and he was knocked on his back into an area where there was dampness and spray from the other waterfall. Bob's getting wet compounded their struggle to keep him alive because hypothermia is a problem in caves, where temperatures range from fifty to sixty degrees.

The next thing Bob knew, he was waking up with no knowledge of where he was—he had been unconscious for about five minutes. He perceived what he slowly processed as bat sounds then heard Pete yelling his name. Pete yelled to him, "You were hit with a rock on your head!" Bob's helmet, along with his carbide lamp, had been knocked off his head and over the edge of the active waterfall. Around Bob's head was a big pool of blood.

When Bob regained consciousness, Pete had already sent Mike for help. Bill was the only one without injury remaining at the bottom of the large pit. Although he was not a novice caver, Bill panicked, thinking that his friend was dead. When Bob came to consciousness, Bill found his courage, plus hope, then went into action. He took charge of settling Pete into a dryer place and wrapping them both with plastic to keep them warm—both Bob and Pete were in enormous pain. Because of his spine injury, Bill was afraid to move Bob out of the damp area of the cave.

They only had one carbide lamp among the three cavers left in the pit. (Pete had an electric lamp which gave no heat.) Bill put the carbide lamp with its flame next to Bob's neck to help stave off hypothermia. Typically, a charge lasts for three hours—this time it miraculously lasted for five hours. Bob was in unbelievable pain and was shivering uncontrollably, then at four hours postinjury the shivering stopped, as well as the pain. This was a very bad sign, meaning that soon (usually within one hour) a coma would follow. At the comatose point, it becomes difficult to bring someone back. (Thankfully, the rescuers arrived with warming equipment at 10:00 pm before Bob sank into a coma. However, I am getting ahead of our story.)

The three young men settled at the bottom of the pit for the long wait. It was hard for Bob to concentrate on anything but the pain, nevertheless, Bill and Bob intermittently prayed together. They had confidence that God would take care of them. Over and over, Bob thought he heard the rescuers, but it was the sound of the waterfall. At one point, Pete saw a mouse, and that kept them all amused for a while. Bill briefly tried singing to encourage them, but the other two quickly silenced him because his crooning left something to be desired.

Meanwhile, Mike had climbed the rest of the one hundred-twenty-foot vertical wall. This was his first time in Buddy Penley's Cave, so he did not know the way out. He tried various paths and marked them with pieces of his clothing to keep track of the ways he had already attempted. (Spelunking with partners is dangerous. Doing so alone is beyond treacherous, especially in such a challenging cave.) The fact that Mike found his way without incident, in a reasonable amount of time, is another amazing testament of God's help to this group. Was he guided by the Holy Spirit in answer to those crying out to God from the bottom of the pit? Mike safely got out and made the emergency call from a nearby farmhouse.

Not coincidentally, at close-by Virginia Tech, a course for cave rescuers, sponsored by the Virginia Association of Volunteer Rescue Squads, was just wrapping up when the call came in that they were all needed for this accident. Around eighty individuals were there, and all were fully trained for just such an incident (another huge, miraculous non-coincidence). This complex rescue in such a difficult cave required a very high number of trained rescue personnel. (There were not nearly enough qualified persons living in the area—maybe thirty at the maximum. Plus, trying to gather these for a rescue would have required time that Bob did not have.)

Many skilled tasks were required to get Bob and Pete out of this extremely challenging terrain. The rescuers had to bring them up the vertical wall on flexible stretcher/backboards using a complex system of ropes and pulleys while another person went up the wall and guided the stretchers to keep them from getting lodged between narrow areas. They also had to get the stretchers back through the extremely confined transitions to the big spaces.

Almost always, even with less complex ones, something goes wrong with cave rescues. Nothing did with this one. Who else but our heavenly Father could bring together exactly those who were needed for what was later hailed in the caving community as a perfect rescue? Bob was helicoptered to a nearby hospital. Pete was taken by ambulance to a Blacksburg hospital. It took sixteen hours from the time of the accident for the rescue to be fully accomplished. Eighteen hours after the rock-fall, Bob was in surgery.

In the meantime, Bob's parents were notified and went to the hospital, expecting the waiting room to be relatively quiet and empty. They were shocked to see so many young people there. As they all waited, the young people huddled in groups and prayed. Bob's dad was already a man of deep, practicing faith. However, Bob's mom, Helga, was still at the place of seeing Christianity as a type of tradition. She was totally fascinated by the young people in the waiting area. When the doctor finally came in and called out "Ulfers Family", everyone in the room stood up. It was the first that Bob's mom understood that all these college kids were there for prayer and support for her son. When the students discovered that these two strangers were Bob's parents, they hurried over to comfort and encourage the couple.

The power of God transformed yet another life through this tragic event. Mrs. Helga Ulfers changed from a traditional church goer to a Christ-follower. She became a lover of Jesus and his Word—she had seen close-up that God sees and cares. Bob's mom collected everything about this story in newspaper clippings and information, plus both his parents wrote to the paper to make sure that God was given the glory for all that He did in this situation. Helga kept the list of the college students who signed up for prayer around the clock for Bob, Pete, and the families. The loving prayers of Bob's Christian community continued throughout the rehab process and as Bob celebrated his twentieth birthday. Mrs. Ulfers cherished everything that showed that God is here on earth with us—hearing, caring, and answering our prayers.

Helga was radically changed—her life shifted in direction. Jesus was alive and real to her. Here is Bob's description of his mom, "She became committed to praying for lots of people. She was known by many as a person of sincere (and simple) trust in God. She prayed Yezmin and me through Cameroon. In the end she had no doubt that God was her Father, and in January when I told her she was dying of stage four cancer, she smiled the biggest smile and recited the twenty-third Psalm. She had become a simple faith-filled child of God."

How many others were affected in this way because of all the miracles that happened on that day? How many down the line had their hearts and lives changed, owing to the mortal wounds of Bob that did not end in death? How many other souls gained eternal life resulting from this chain of events? Probably thousands or more heard the word of God as Bob and his wife translated the Bible into one of Cameroon's native languages. Bob was prepared for his later ministry by this dire and agonizing period during college.

After hearing Bob speak about his caving experience, I asked this question, "What on earth would motivate anyone to go under the ground where there is total darkness and to do dangerous and challenging climbs,
including dropping down a one-hundred-and-twenty-foot cliff?"

Here was his answer, "Caving is not for everyone. For me to view these huge underground glorious rooms of fantastic cave formations after crawling through mud lined narrow passages is like entering into a sacred chamber designed by God, like snowflakes or flowers or mushrooms – always new, different and beautiful."

How was Bob's life after this? I would love to tell you that he was completely healed without any leftover effects from his accident, but I cannot. Recovery was slow and very painful. Where his skull was crushed, there is now metal and plastic mesh, which replaced the part of the bone the surgeons removed. He has some neck pain and limitation, especially if he mistakenly falls asleep sitting up. Although it is fully functional, half of Bob's left arm is numb. He also "types funny" (his words). Yet, Bob is a walking, talking, breathing miracle.

Let me tell you the most amazing part. Bob understandably went through some soul-searching after the accident. He had deep and serious talks with God. Eventually, he took a hike alone and spent lots of time in honest dialogue saying things like, "God, you let this happen to me, and I don't know if I want to stay with you."

Eventually, he reached the same conclusion that Christ's disciples did in John 6:60-71. "So, Jesus said to the twelve, "Do you want to go away as well?" Simon Peter answered him, "Lord, to whom shall we go? You have the words of eternal life, and we have believed, and have come to know, that you are the Holy One of God."

Bob and Yezmin met at Virginia Tech before the accident but barely knew each other. After Bob's injury, they began spending lots of time together (classes, church, Intervarsity, Missions Group, etc.) because Yezmin and Bob were the only ones at Virginia Tech who had an interest in Bible translation. They married on Sept 3, 1983. Bob is convinced that Yezmin would never have agreed to marry the prideful, pre-accident version of himself.

After this story took place, Bob and his wife became missionaries for Wycliffe Bible Translators in Cameroon for thirty years. Wycliffe (known overseas as SIL) was founded by William Cameron Townsend, who was an inspiration for Bob Ulfers. He had hopes to meet this great man, however Townsend died on April 23, 1982, while Bob was still recovering from his injuries. The goal of Wycliffe is to translate the New Testament (and sometimes the Old Testament) into all languages of the world. Currently, that includes digital and audio versions as well. This attracted Bob because of the definitive finish line and the continuance of eternal seeds for generations to come. There are about six thousand languages in the world and still many translations needed.

If you are as ignorant as I was about the country of their mission, Cameroon, know that it is at the junction of western and central Africa. It became an independent nation on January 1, 1960. Before that, it was mainly a colony of France (and some of Great Britain). It is a small, and not very safe, country with French and English as official languages. (Bob and Yezmin did have some perilous times there during their ministry, but God always protected them.) The French and English languages have been used by the government and schools since World War 1. Karang is one of hundreds of native languages of Cameroon. Bob and his wife translated the New Testament into that language—it was published and audio-recorded in 2020. At that point, Bob and Yezmin's calling for that particular purpose was completed.

Here is Bob's statement about the impact of this work, "The Karang language is spoken by about twenty thousand people and understood by about one-hundred thousand.

There are over two thousand languages on the continent of Africa. There is revival taking place today among the young Karang people." My personal question is this: How much did Bob's miracle play a part in what is now a revival? Our willingness to be refined in the fire may open doors and accomplish eternal purposes.

Bob eventually told God that he would even be willing to go through it all again to get to the point of humility and dependence that was brought about by this event. Through this intense training course, Bob reached the point of submission to God that enabled his life to be eternally significant. Bob was ready to be used for God's purposes as a missionary to Cameroon or in any way that God directed.

Bob and Yezmin are back in the United States now (Yezmin in 2018 and Bob after wrapping up loose ends in 2020). They are driving buses and waiting on the Lord to show them the significant and eternal purposes that He has for the second half of their lives. Bob is still in touch with the Karang community and developed a Karang website to make the scriptures and other materials available to encourage them.

Bob asked for my perspective on what this and the other miracle stories have done for me personally. I will answer this in total transparency. When a friend, asked me to recount some of my miracles, I was in a time of discouragement. I had been living in lots of pain and could see no end in sight—privately I asked God many times if it was just time for him to take me home. Also, I had no assignment from God and felt like my life was just drifting along without real purpose. The writing of this book, telling my miracles and hearing others, has been a refresher course for me on the very foundational fact that God is always here—he continually sees, hears, cares, and responds. When we don't recognize that truth, it is from blindness and deafness on our parts because of deliberate choices we make. These miracle stories have given me reawakened hope and expectation, plus a willingness to wait on God in knowledge that he is ever active in our lives. They have also reopened my eyes to the miracles, big and little, all around us.

Jonah 2: 4. "I sank down to the very roots of the mountains. I was imprisoned in the earth, whose gates lock shut forever. But you, O Lord my God, snatched me from the jaws of death!"

Psalm 34: 17-18. "When the righteous cry for help, the Lord hears and delivers them out of all their troubles. The Lord is near to the brokenhearted and saves the crushed in spirit."

Father, thank You for using this horrific event to produce a godly and effective minister for your purposes. Thank You for maturing Bob so that he could serve you. Thank You for every detail of this complex and amazing set of miracles that you performed for your beloved child. Thank You that you are not finished with Bob and Yezmin yet, but You have more great purposes for them. In Jesus name, Amen

Peace throughout the Danger

In 2019, two months after having a stroke (cerebral vascular accident), Karl (not his real name) was to travel to Charleston, West Virginia, to appear in a commercial for his company. Because of his recent stroke, the plan was for him to travel to Morgantown and to ride on to Charleston with Rick, another salesman who was also to be filmed for the commercial. They were having intermittent, low-keyed conversation, when suddenly, about one hour south of

Morgantown, Karl noticed that they were a mere twelve inches from hitting the guardrail. After discovering that Rick had become unconscious, Karl grabbed the wheel to keep from crashing. Immediately, he prayed, "God, I need your help."

The amazing thing was that there was no panic and no fear—Karl was completely at peace. The car was in cruise-control going seventy miles per hour, but everything seemed to slow down. Karl kept control of the wheel while calmly checking traffic. A white car passed them without incident, then the way was completely clear. The odd thing was that the road seemed perfectly straight, although Karl knew there were very few straight sections on Interstate-79 in that area.

Between Karl and the driver's side, there was a large console blocking Karl from getting his foot across to the brake. Without any yelling or alarm, Karl began calmly telling Rick over and over, "Rick, I need you to put your foot on the brake."

Finally, Rick woke with a start, mumbling, "What? What?" Karl told him to hit the brake and explained that he had passed out. After that, they were able to pull over to the side of the road safely.

"Are you diabetic? Do you have a heart condition?" Karl asked his colleague. Both replies were negative. Rick wanted to return to Morgantown to a familiar medical facility, so Karl drove them back there. When they were five miles away, Karl called Rick's parents so they could meet them at the hospital.

After Rick's discharge from the hospital, he called Karl to convey to him what the doctors said: Rick's fainting was caused by a vasovagal response. A vasovagal response is a reaction to some stimuli which causes a sudden drop in blood pressure which thereby brings on fainting. This can be set off by a variety of triggers, but Rick did not have any prior medical history of this condition. The doctors conjectured that Rick's apprehension over making the commercial may have been the trigger.

The perfect peace that passes understanding overwhelmed Karl that day, keeping him calm and clear-headed. After the incident, Rick kept reiterating to Karl, "You saved my life."

Karl made it perfectly clear that was not the case. "Rick, God saved your life, not me." There was no doubt in Karl's mind that he had seen a miracle in which God intervened, saving both men.

Philippians 4:6 "The Lord is near! Do not be anxious about anything. Instead, in every situation with prayer and petition with thanksgiving, tell your requests to God. And the peace that surpasses all understanding will guard your hearts and minds in Christ Jesus."

Psalm 46:1 "God is our refuge and strength, an ever present help in trouble."

Lord, thank You for your protection and for the peace that You bestow upon us. In Jesus name, Amen

God Cares for Those Who Trust in Him

Angela Usas is an American girl fluent in Spanish, who studied abroad in Spain for her junior year of college, then returned there for a period in 2002 and 2003. This story took place in May of 2003 when Angela was twenty-three years old. Her Spanish boyfriend, named Ivan, made plans for the two of them to hike in the Pyrenees. The only problem was that Ivan was a little spacey, which gave his friends concerns about Ivan's and Angela's safety. Ivan's friends came over and checked through the items they were putting in their backpacks to make sure they had what they needed. Unfortunately, all of them missed the fact that Angela did not pack sunglasses.

Ivan and Angela left for their hike and discovered (when they drove to the bottom of the mountain where they parked the car) that there were two feet of snow where they would be hiking. Angela did not have her sunglasses but did not think that was a real problem. Their plan was to hike to a hostel to sleep that night, but the deep snow made them take longer so they did not make it.

Thankfully, Ivan remembered a cave from previous hiking, and he took them there to spend the night. The cave was small with an opening that was about three feet high in the side of the mountain.

When they got in the cave, Angela's eyes started burning and watering terribly. The pain was non-stop, and her vision was also affected. The ultraviolet light from the bright sun had reflected from the snow to Angela's unprotected eyes and caused snow blindness. This is essentially a sunburn of the eyes. It can be minimal or very severe—in Angela's case it was severe. She could not sleep because of the pain.

Angela instinctively knew that she had to protect her eyes from more exposure, so the next morning, Ivan left without her to hike to the hostel to find help. Angela stayed in the cave, trying to let her eyes heal. Ivan did not pass any people on his way to the hostel. Much to his dismay, when he reached the hostel, it was closed. On his way back to the cave, he only met one couple. He told them about Angela and her eye damage as well as the location of the cave, asking them to send help.

Ivan got back to the cave after being gone about five hours. They settled down to rest, and Angela could now get some sleep because the pain had receded a bit. Neither Ivan nor Angela was sure that the couple would send help or that they could even give accurate directions for a rescue team to find the cave. To their huge surprise and joy, they were awakened that night by the loud sound of a helicopter landing outside of the cave. A rescue mission had been sent to get Angela!

The helicopter crew would only take Angela, so Ivan had to hike down the mountain. They flew Angela to a nearby Spanish hospital in a town that Angela did not know. They told her that she needed treatment because her eyes had been severely burned by the ultraviolet rays, and that would involve having ointment in her eyes and covering them for twenty-four hours. The hard part was that she had to be discharged from the hospital after the ointment and coverings were applied to her eyes. She needed someone to take care of her and a place to stay. Ivan would not be down the mountain until the next day.

The hospital made a call to the Civil Guard and told them about Angela's situation. (The Civil Guard is one branch of the police force in Spain. In general, the Civil Guard handles rural areas, and the National Police oversee urban areas.) A Civil Guardsman named Raimundo volunteered to give Angela a place to stay and to take care of her until Ivan got back from his return journey. Raimundo came to the hospital and met Angela before they put the dressings on her eyes that would make her functionally blind for twenty-four hours. Next, they put the ointment in her eyes and covered them, and Angela left the hospital with a complete stranger!

Raimundo was stationed for a time near the hospital where Angela was treated--his family was not with him during this period he was serving. Thankfully, Raimundo spoke of his wife and four-year-old daughter—just hearing that he was a family man made Angela feel more comfortable. Raimundo took Angela to where he was housed and made her snacks and meals and even helped her to eat. The next morning, he drove her to the Civil Guard station where they met Ivan.

Angela made it safely through her ordeal, but when she has current eye exams, the doctors can still see the burn scars from the ultraviolet light exposure. Thankfully, it has not had any long-term effects on her vision.

Friends predicted that Angela would get a whopping bill for the helicopter ride and for the hospitalization--she has never received a bill for either. Since then, Angela sends a Christmas card to Raimundo every year. She still views him as her guardian angel and 'God's love in the flesh'.

Did Angela pray during her pain and hardship? She is sure that she must have, but what she really remembers is just trusting God. She had no fear or panic about her eyes, about being left alone in a cave in the Pyrenees, or about going with a strange man and letting him take care of her. Wow! Such faith and trust!

Did this experience change Angela? She was impacted, especially by Raimundo and his kindness.

If I had to choose a word to describe Angela, it is 'kind'. She loves to serve and does it without a second thought. She took care of her father-in-law as he was dying. She champions underdogs and always has a cause that she is supporting. Did Raimundo's guardian angel example stir up some of this in Angela? I believe so.

Nahum 1:7 "The Lord is good, a refuge in times of trouble. He cares for those who trust in him."

Father, thank you for tender hearts like Raimundo's. Thank you for provision and protection like you gave to Angela. Thank You for preserving her vision. In Jesus' name, Amen

Angels Unaware

This story will be anonymous at the request of the principal characters. The names are changed, but the story is completely true.

Jack had taught his son, Bobby, to drive on their family truck. When Bobby was ready to get his license, his oldest brother, offered up his old, small car to be Bobby's first vehicle. (His brother was getting a new one.) Jack bought this used Toyota Celica for Bobby's first car.

Jack and his son were on their way to pick up Bobby's driver's license with the young man in the driver's seat, testing out his newfound skills in his newly acquired Celica. Bobby had passed his test but was still a totally inexperienced driver. They were driving on a busy road with lots of traffic and approached a four-way stop. Young Bobby scanned traffic diligently but lacked the expertise to double-check his blind spot. As he pulled into the intersection, another car came from the passenger's side direction and T-boned into the side of the Celica, right where Jack was sitting. The door crumpled into Jack so that he was wedged in by the crunched metal.

From the moment that Jack saw the car coming towards him, he saw everything in slow motion, but the crash itself knocked him unconscious. When he came to, he was having difficulty breathing and could not move except to turn his head just enough to see his son. Bobby had blood on his face, and Jack's overwhelming desire was to know that his son was okay and protected from further injury in the busy thoroughfare.

Miraculously, in the car two vehicles behind them were two EMT's, a man and a woman. The woman came to the passenger side where Jack was wedged, and asked, "What do you need me to do?"

Jack had to settle down and slow his panicked breathing so that he was able to answer, because one lung was collapsed from the injury. As soon as he was able, Jack replied, "Take care of my son, and get him out of the car so that he does not get hurt worse." God's gift of the Holy Spirit in Jack put an overwhelming concern for his son foremost on his heart--the Spirit superseded the survival instinct with a love that laid down his own life for his son's.

The female EMT seemed to understand that Jack could not let them attend to his own injuries until he knew that his son was okay. Soon, they had Bobby sitting in the grass by the side of the road, out of harm's way. He had a bump on his head, but he was all right.

Not so Jack, who was very badly injured! The door had crumpled into him so much that they had to remove him with the Jaws of Life. Even when the door was finally opened, Jack still could not be pulled out—they had to lift him out by his belt, straight upward.

They carefully took him to the hospital while his wife was notified. When they wheeled Jack in on a gurney, he passed right by his wife. She saw him but didn't even recognize him because Jack was such a bloody, beat-up mess. He had a head injury, a punctured lung, and his right hip was shattered to smithereens.

It was a hard recovery but a miraculous one. The surgeon who patched up Jack's hip was beyond amazing. Jack still has his original hip, and he now approaches seventy years old. Jack is convinced that the EMT's were angels put there just for him and that the medical people were also miracle workers. It is true that there are angels around us because the Bible speaks of it. I totally believe those two individuals who helped after the accident were angels put there to help this precious and beloved man.

Hebrews 13:2 "Be not forgetful to entertain strangers: for thereby some have entertained angels unaware."

Thank You, Lord, for protecting and healing this special man with your helpers. In Jesus' name, Amen

A Mother's Prayers

As a mother of three wild boys myself, this story wrenches my heart. Karen is the amazing and faithful mom in this story, and Michael is her wild-boy son. Karen is one of those people to whom everyone turns when life goes into a downward spiral. She really hears and sees what is going on in a way few people can. Karen grasps the true need and then immediately carries the crux of the problem or crisis to the only one who can help--she prays to the one true God. I mean she REALLY PRAYS!

There have been many admirable people in my life, but Karen is up there near the top. She is truly a woman of noble character. We met in the summer of 2012, and during that first meeting, I told her about a small group that Lee and I were trying to start. It was amusing because everyone whom we invited turned us down, and we were ready to scrap the idea. Just moments after meeting Karen, I mentioned the small group that was not coming together and Karen said, "Could I be in it?" It seemed like it would end up with just Karen, Lee, and me meeting together, however this group ended up being a good sized, cross-denominational, strong assemblage of gifted individuals with depth and faith. It is still going strong nine years later, but now Karen is the leader.

A year before I met Karen, she had a perfect storm of events in her life. Her youngest son, Mark, had developed Crohn's Disease after getting a flu vaccination. He was quite sick and not yet stabilized with a definitive plan of action. Karen was still helping him to navigate through the maze of options and treatment when a second big incident occurred.

Karen's oldest son, Michael was selected to be in a study abroad program for collegiate musicians. These musically gifted college students were to study under prestigious musicians and participate in several performances in Vienna, Austria. Michael played bass trombone and was roommates during the trip with a trombone player who attended University of Illinois. Michael was twenty-one years old at that time and was in the stage of life when drinking with his friends was an important pastime.

The father of Michael's roommate for the excursion had a lot of practical knowledge about ways to stay safe in Austria while they were there. Before the trip, he met with his son, with Michael, and with Karen to talk about cautions to put in practice to stay out of harm's way. One thing he advised was to be very careful about drinking the alcoholic drinks because they are more potent than in the United States.

This musical excursion involved a two-week indoctrination period in which the young musicians learned as much language and culture as possible. After that they would have a week of performances. At the end of the indoctrination interval, Karen and Michael had a Skype call to catch up with each other. During this conversation, Karen reiterated the warning to her son about drinking.

A group of the kids, including Michael, decided to go out to blow off steam after their two-week learning period. They started off the evening by drinking a bottle of rum before they even left the hotel. Next the kids went to a karaoke bar which, of course, involved more drinking. About half of the group returned to the hotel after that, but for a small number of boys the evening was just beginning. This group seemed to consist of the more athletic and adventurous young men. Their abilities, in combination with the alcohol, made for a dangerous competition of daring feats. The sport that they were doing was Parkour, which is defined as: the sport of traversing environmental obstacles by running, climbing, or leaping rapidly and efficiently.[20] These obstacles that are negotiated are usually at heights, not on the ground. This is not a safe sport when sober, much less so after drinking. There have been numerous deaths in Parkours, even when the participants are trained and sober.

The group of guys climbed a scaffolding and were doing tricks from ten feet up then landing on the concrete below. One of the young men did a back flip from the scaffold and landed on his feet on the concrete. Michael decided to try the same thing, but instead of landing on his feet, he landed on his head. Miraculously, he did not die upon impact!

The other boys called an ambulance and Michael was taken to a Vienna hospital. Michael was seriously injured. He had a basilar skull fracture with cerebral spinal fluid (CSF) and blood flowing from his ears and into his eye sockets. In twelve to thirty percent of the cases in which the base of the skull is fractured, there is a leak of CSF.[21] This often shows up as clear fluid dripping from the nose. Michael's leak was significant with immediate signs of the drainage—it was detectable in the fluid coming from his ears and nose (the blood and CSF mixture), and he also had very black eyes from the flow into his eye sockets.

When Karen got the call about what happened to Michael, she was walking to the baseball field for her other son's game. The head of the international music program (that Michael was part of) called her from Vienna and told her what had happened. She began shaking violently, praying, and running all at the same time—she expended all her energy in a desperate attempt to reach her husband quickly at the baseball field. Rattled beyond control, Karen prayed again and again, "Lord, please save him!" This began her (almost) 24/7 period of prayer for her son. All her strength and passion were poured into constant crying out to God for her son's life. Once Karen reached her husband in his car at the baseball field, she pounded on the window because he was on the phone. When her husband understood the desperate nature of what was happening, they drove back to call the doctor in Vienna, Austria.

What the Austrian neurologist told Karen and her husband (in very broken English mixed with German) was not to come to Vienna for three days. Those three days of waiting were absolute hell. As they waited, they made plans about what to do. Karen did not feel like she could leave Mark, their youngest, who was still very sick with Crohn's disease. Scott was going to have to go alone and leave his busy career as a navy endodontist. During communications with the doctors, they were told what was happening, however the language barrier made this quite difficult. God provided through the father of Michael's roommate. He knew the mentor of the music program in Austria, and he contacted this man who became the interpreter between

Karen, her husband, and the doctors. This seemed like another provision from God.

There are two major ways in treating cerebral spinal fluid leaks: conservative management or surgical repair.[22] There are some different surgical procedures used, but the hospital, where Michael was, chose the conservative method. Michael was not able to be moved to another facility because of the fragile state of his skull and brain, so the strategy of this hospital became basically the only possible choice for him. Flying Michael home was not an option because of what the pressurized plane cabin could do to Michael's healing brain—the injury had caused air bubbles in his brain and the pressure in the plane could work havoc on this. This locked-in strategy for treatment became another part of this miracle. Michael's body, given protection and rest, used its God-given ability to heal itself without disturbance, thanks to the hospital where Michael ended up for his recovery.

Here was the system of the Vienna hospital: Michael got no medications at all; the hospital staff kept him still and gave him lots of fluids intravenously; plus, they carefully monitored his vitals. Michael had initial pain after his injury, but this was due to detoxing the heavy alcohol content in his blood. For the head injury, he needed no pain meds because the brain has no pain receptors.

When Scott arrived in Vienna and saw his son, he was shocked at how terrible he looked. There was severe bruising, especially around Michael's eyes. Michael was not eating at all, and when Scott reported to Karen, it was a dismal account. Communication across countries by phone was difficult at that time—eventually they found an international service plan, which helped somewhat. Scott was in Vienna for three weeks and was getting concerned about work-related things, but there still was no option to move Michael. Finally, the air bubbles in Michael's brain had decreased to only one small bubble, and the doctors consented to let Michael fly home if he got a CT scan immediately after getting back. Karen arranged with the navy hospital for Michael's care—the follow up CT scan still showed the small air bubble but no increase in damage.

Michael was allowed no activity for one month, plus no trombone playing. After five weeks, he was permitted to play basketball. When college started in August, he was approved to return. He did not miss one day of school.

Interestingly, this was not the first time Michael was preserved by God's hand. At eight years old, another child in his class in school threw a newly sharpened pencil and hit him right in the eye, penetrating his cornea and lens. He had emergency surgery the next day, but the doctors could not give a prognosis. Losing his sight was a real possibility. Michael had another four surgeries, then a fifth after developing a cataract in the same eye.

Amazingly, miraculously, he now has twenty/twenty vision in that eye.

I have met Michael a few times—he is now a lawyer. He seems to be a very kind-hearted young man. Just as he was before the accident, Michael is still very athletic and fit. The only lasting effect that he had from this accident is that he has a diminished sense of smell and taste (his tasting ability has since improved). Did this accident drive him into the arms of God? Not yet, but I have great expectations. Angels cushioned his fall and hastened his recovery.

If a mother's prayers were counted, I think the ones for Michael are reaching into the millions. It is my opinion that God has great plans for him.

Proverbs 31:30 "Charm can be deceptive, and beauty doesn't last, but a woman who fears and reverences God shall be greatly praised. Praise her for the many fine things she does. These good deeds of hers shall bring her honor and recognition from people of importance."

Father, thank You for the perseverance in prayer of a good mother. Thank You when she will not give up or lose hope. Thank You that she will keep praying for her kids until her dying day when she has no more breath left to pray. In Jesus name, Amen

He Will Give His Angels Charge Over You

Upon meeting Keith and Jay, it was obvious from their words and actions that Christ is the focus of their lives. Their love for Jesus seems to naturally bubble up in what they say and how they act. When both young men found out that I was writing a book about miracles, they excitedly told me some miracle stories. I will relate one of those events.

Keith Schrock is a stone-mason contractor who works with his associate whom I will call Jay. These guys are devoted and exceptional workers, focused on doing excellent jobs as quickly as possible. They have been doing stonework for us this past week, and we have been blown away by their work ethic. They drive about two hours to get to our home, get there around 7:00 am and often work well into the evening, then still have the two hour trip to get back home.

Recently, Keith and Jay were doing a job close to their hometown of Berlin, Ohio. They were working outside on a scaffold that was three levels high--that is equal to about two house-stories. They were getting towards the end of the day and were running out of daylight but had a light rigged up to help them see. Keith was on the top level of the scaffold, moving boards around to get everything battened down to leave it overnight. He did not have safety railings up because he had to be able to move around freely.

Jay was moving things from the ground up to the scaffold with a telehandler, which is also known as a telescopic forklift. He had reached the point of very low visibility because it was getting dark. However, Keith did not realize how difficult Jay's job was becoming in the fading light. He trusted that the light they had set up was enough for continuing to finish up with safety.

Keith was moving a piece of heavy plywood, and he was facing towards the building with his back to the open drop-off from the scaffold. Meanwhile, Jay brought the forklift up to the scaffold to transfer materials from the ground. He misjudged in the bad lighting and bumped the platform with the lift with a hard jolt. Keith (holding the heavy plywood) was knocked backward towards thin air and a two-story fall to the ground. There was nothing he could do to save or stop himself from falling backwards to certain injury or possible death.

Miraculously, Keith felt a hand on his back giving him a push from behind—this put him back into an upright position where he regained his balance and was safe. The hand stayed on his back until he was steady on his feet again. God had given angels watch over him—an angel gave him an actual push from behind so that he did not fall off the three-level-high scaffold.

Psalm 91:1. "For He shall give His angels charge over you to keep you in all your ways."

Father, thank You for the angels whom you have given to keep watch over us and protect us. We are so grateful, and we will look for them in our lives, day-to-day. Help us to be aware of all the miracles You do for us in our everyday lives. In Jesus' name, Amen

Defeating Goliath

A gentle and soft-spoken mother and son entered my life in 2008 --I will refer to them as Joy and John. At the time I met her, Joy and her eight-year-old son, John, lived in the same village as me. Joy was functioning as a single mom and homeschooling her son after a divorce due to her ex-husband's infidelity.

Joy and I met after she was diagnosed with breast cancer. Along with our church counselor, I visited to encourage Joy and to help her deal with all that comes along with such a diagnosis. (Not long before this, I had been diagnosed with breast cancer myself and had gone through treatment.) Meeting Joy and John was a blessing to me-they were both such kind and gentle people.

Joy had an extremely aggressive form of breast cancer-mastectomies, chemo, and radiation were all recommended as treatment. It would be a brutal regimen to go through, and she had no one to help her. (Her son was still very young at the time.)

Joy was from Czech Republic originally and went to occasional gatherings of people from Czech Republic and neighboring Slavic countries. At those sessions, she met a man whom I will call Harvey. Harvey was handsome, seemed very in love with Joy, and appeared to radiate kindness. He told Joy that he was a fervent believer just as his grandma had been. (He knew that this was the highest priority with Joy). As Harvey was repeatedly asking Joy to marry him, he presented himself as a Union mason and a naturalized United States citizen. He knew about her breast cancer and the grueling treatment that Joy would receive, and Harvey told her that he wanted to offer support. Harvey pressured Joy to marry him, saying that she could not go through this without his help. She never asked for his assistance—the idea was totally from him. He especially pressed home the point that John needed Harvey to be an extra parent as his mom went through treatment.

Five days before Joy had the double mastectomy surgery, she and Harvey married. They did not tell her friends until after the marriage was a done deal. We were all taken aback, but later thought Harvey might be a gift from God to help Joy through this horrible time.

Harvey was extremely good looking, charming, and skilled at communicating. Despite coming from Czech Republic, he had adapted well to living in the United States. Initially, it appeared to be a match made in heaven.

From the outside, it looked as if Harvey was a very kind man. He took Joy to her surgery and helped with everything. Joy found out later that Harvey took control of her phone while she was in the hospital. He deleted messages from her friends and blocked their ability to contact her. He even sent bogus emails in Joy's name without her knowledge. Joy found out about this six weeks later when a good friend asked why she never answered her messages. Her friend had tried to reach out when Joy had her surgery and hospitalization.

When Joy and Harvey were both tied up with her medical procedures, I babysat for John, and each time I saw Harvey, he seemed like a doting husband and a good substitute dad. It seemed like he could be a good friend and support to John, as well as an ideal spouse to Joy.

After the cancer diagnosis, Joy researched and decided on the Gerson protocol to help her regain her health (a rigorous diet and lifestyle regimen which is extremely labor intensive). Initially, not only did Harvey pitch in to help with the cooking, juicing, and workings of this program, but also, he decided that he would eat the diet to support Joy. It seemed like Harvey was sent from God for this very difficult time in Joy's and John's life. Very quickly, however, Harvey started using his assistance to manipulate Joy. He constantly demanded money, citizenship, and that Joy and John comply with his wishes for him to give any help at all.

Pretty soon, cracks that were visible to the outside world started showing up in the household. The ideal husband and stepdad façade started to crumble. When I went to visit, it was obvious that Harvey was hypercritical of John. "John, did you line up your shoes by the door? Are you sitting perfectly straight? You left some crumbs on the table and need to clean them up." Although John was extremely well behaved, as well as being neater and more helpful than any child I had ever met, he could not please his stepfather. Harvey also began criticizing Joy publicly as well as privately-- Joy and John felt like their home had turned into a war zone.

At some point, Joy realized that John was being negatively affected by having Harvey in their home. She sought help from a Christian counselor, who put rules in place that only Joy could institute John's discipline. Harvey was to stop with his negative comments and criticisms of John. I noticed that after Harvey came into their home, John began stuttering at times and seemed nervous. Previously, he was a calm and self-assured child—it was very disturbing to see the fear that crept into his young life.

Joy's friends did not know what to do about the situation— Joy was determined to make the marriage work. We started seeing fear in Joy as well as John— there was no peace to be found in their home with Harvey there. We kept asking if Harvey was physically hurting either Joy or John. Joy said that other than mean words, he was not abusive. She was embarrassed to tell of the real situation—she thought that she was 'turning the other cheek' like Jesus spoke of in the Bible. (Joy found out later that hiding the cruelty and abuse is a common response to such a situation.) At the time it was all happening, Joy thought that with prayer and the help of Jesus, Harvey could become a good husband and father.

A metamorphosis in Harvey never happened. Harvey was not a Union mason with a job--he never worked or contributed resources while married to Joy. He was not a United States citizen—he tried to use Joy to get his citizenship. He was not a kind man who loved Joy and wanted to help her-- Harvey was a gold-digger preying on weak, ill, and helpless people. I found out later that Harvey was not only mentally abusive, but he also physically abused Joy. She kept silent in hopes of saving the marriage until she saw him for the destructive person he was—a narcissist, and possibly even a sociopath.

Harvey started demanding more and more money and began draining the savings that Joy had received in settlement from her previous divorce. He kept his condo and used Joy's money to make payments—he used the condo as his escape route when things got uncomfortable for him. He pushed to have his name put on the deed of the house, and he constantly demanded that Joy sponsor him to be a United States citizen. As time elapsed, he got progressively more threatening with his demands.

Thankfully, Joy had the foresight not to put him on the deed and never would consent to be part of the process of making him a United States citizen. At some point, Joy woke up and saw that she was being used. This was in large part because her church friends helped her to see the truth of the situation.

One friend, who is a nurse, was suspicious because Joy's health was constantly deteriorating. It turned out that Harvey was slowly poisoning Joy by adding wormwood powder to her food when he was helping with the cooking. Wormwood is an herbal medicine often used on a short-term basis for killing parasites, but it Is poisonous if continued for very long. Joy's health went downhill to the point of not being able to walk—she needed a wheelchair to function. (Thankfully, a lot of this has since reversed, and Joy regained much of her health after her ordeal was over.)

Joy was married to Harvey for eight years and getting him out of her life was like David battling Goliath. Finally, Joy made it clear to her friends and her church that she was being abused. She did not have a lot of resources to pay her way out of her situation. Her husband had depleted her savings and built up his own bank account using Joy's money.

Her friends and the church mobilized to help Joy and John. A father of John's friend at church, whom I will

call Don, had seen that John needed an advocate and protector against his stepdad. He made himself a presence so that Harvey could not freely bully his family. Also, her friends from church encouraged Joy to let the police know of the abusive situation and to change the locks.

Joy could not afford a lawyer, but God provided a lawyer from the church who helped with filing for divorce. Things gradually started to move in the direction of removing Harvey from their lives.

Harvey had stolen Joy's money for his own purposes: to pay off his condo, to buy a car, and to buy lots of stuff for himself. Joy also found out later (through his computer communications) that Harvey had a mistress back in Czech Republic to whom he sent money and gifts throughout his marriage to Joy. There was no getting any of the lost money back—Joy just wanted Harvey out of their lives completely, so that she and John could start to heal from the trauma he brought into their existence.

Even after changing the locks and calling the police, Harvey continued to bother Joy and John. He would come to the door and knock, hoping to wear them down. There were also constant threatening phone messages. He drove by the house and even tried to come in the back entrance. He called Joy constantly, attempting to convince her to let him back in the house and into their lives.

Harvey kept saying to Joy, "You are going to die." Joy felt terrorized and paralyzed with fear for her safety, but the police could not help without a restraining order. Church friends pressed Joy to go after the restraining order, however this meant getting a good lawyer and going to court. A lawyer, whom I will call Darlene, stepped up to help. She offered her assistance, pro bono, to get a restraining order so that Joy and John could feel safe again. Darlene was a miraculous part of the process of finally getting Harvey out of Joy and John's lives.

Darlene had been in a marriage with a narcissist herself and knew how devastating it was. She was working as a topnotch corporate lawyer at that time—she did not practice divorce law or seek a restraining order for anyone until Joy became her friend. Because of her own experience, Darlene was very wise in dealing with bullies like Harvey, however Joy was Darlene's first case of helping an abused woman. (Darlene has now switched from corporate law to dedicating her life to assist women like Joy—that has become her life's goal. She eventually wrote a book about dealing with narcissists, sociopaths, and psychopaths. Joy's story is in that book.)

Darlene arranged a time for Joy to go before the judge in court. Harvey had hired a very aggressive and ruthless lawyer with a reputation of getting his clients what they wanted. Darlene set it up for me to go to court with them to testify on Joy's behalf. She also asked Don, the father at church who had been a quiet defender of Joy and John, to go on court day. Darlene told Don and me not to worry— she would handle everything. We did not need to prepare a testimony--we just had to go along and trust her.

On the day of court, Joy and I rode together. We sat together first in a hallway, then in a courtroom as Darlene communicated off and on with Harvey's lawyer. We watched as numerous cases were settled by the judge, who seemed to be very fair. By the time most cases came to him, the parties and lawyers had already worked things out.

That was not true in the case of Joy and Harvey. Their lawyers kept talking intermittently right up until it was time for the case to come before the judge. As we sat in the courtroom, we had to be completely silent. Harvey kept looking at Joy in an intimidating way, but she did not return any of his looks. He also kept glancing at Don and me—it seemed that he was wondering what we were going to say when we testified. The atmosphere was oppressive and scary for Joy--I could feel her shaking.

Finally, I took Joy's hand and whispered, "Let's pray!" We both prayed silently but each of us felt the power of God descend on that courtroom. We had been praying about the whole situation for a long time, but it felt like the Holy Spirit showed up and dealt with this abusive bully in that moment.

Joy's case was next on the docket. After our prayer, Joy stopped trembling. Harvey's lawyer motioned to Joy's lawyer, and they asked the judge to wait as they went out to the hallway to talk once again.

We did not know what to expect, but Joy's lawyer came back in and said, "It is finished." She took us out to the hall to explain that Harvey instructed his lawyer to concede and accept the restraining order. The restraining order commanded no contact for life.

God defeated Goliath with a mighty blow! He defended this gentle woman and her son using His people in various ways. It took the slingshot wound to the head when the Holy Spirit came whooshing down in that courtroom to finish it off.

The church still helped Joy and John as they pieced their lives back together after that. They helped to put a security system in her home so that they could feel safe. Church friends helped to pack up Harvey's stuff and went with her to the front of the police station to the drop off where Harvey would pick it up. (Joy's attorney reminded Joy never to encounter Harvey alone per the conditions of the restraining order.) Her friends from the church also helped her to get her house ready to sell.

In the years since then, Joy and John have been gradually healing and slowly rebuilding their lives. It is a painstaking process, but they can always look back to when God defeated Goliath for them.

1 Samuel 17: 45-46 "David said to the Philistine, "You come against me with sword and spear and javelin, but I come against you in the name of the Lord Almighty, the God of the armies of Israel, whom you have defied. This day the Lord will deliver you into my hands, and I'll strike you down and cut off your head.""

Lord, You are our loving Father. When we have enemies who come against us, we can turn to You. You provide for every step of the battle. You defeat Goliath when we cannot with our own strength. Thank you. In Jesus name, Amen

A Life Preserved Again and Again

There are those individuals who have lots of miracles in their lives, otherwise they would not still be alive. Erik Abel is one of those people—he is my quite exceptional nephew. To quote this young man's father, "Erik has been pushed through the knothole backwards" (meaning he has had lots of tough things happen to him). Erik is one of those extremely rare persons who is kind, empathetic, and very insightful. Some of his hard knocks may have helped to shape him that way.

When Erik was about one year old, he was in one of those circular walkers in which the baby sits in a sling-type seat and can push himself around on wheels using his legs. (I am not sure they even make them anymore, because they were not very safe).

This active baby managed to push himself over to the basement door, which inadvertently had been left unlatched. Erik managed to get the door open enough to squeeze through, and down he went, tumbling the span of the uncarpeted steps towards certain injury or death on the cement floor below. Rather than the catastrophic injury or worse that could have occurred in in landing on the unfinished basement concrete floor, he slipped through the railing and ended up landing sitting upright on the only cushion in the basement. He was unhurt. How is that for a miracle? I would say that is starting life out with a bang.

Later, when Erik was about five years old, he slipped when going over a relatively high footbridge and fell into a creek bed face-down on the rocky bottom below. It was a significant height, and this little guy landed on his vulnerable chest and tummy on some jagged stones.

Both parents were at work, but the babysitter was with him as the fall occurred. It first appeared that Erik only had 'the breath knocked out of him'. Thankfully, the sitter had the wisdom to contact his mom and dad who rushed to his aid. Erik's mom immediately knew this was a serious injury. Erik was in such great pain that his dad had to carry him to the car—he was unable to walk at all. Mom and Dad took him to the hospital and found out that he had ruptured his spleen.

Miraculously, after a series of blood transfusions and a nine-day hospital stay under the care of a great team of clinicians (and perhaps some guardian angels), young Erik got to keep his spleen and did not have surgery. The bleeding stopped and imaging revealed a 'split' that was resolving without further intervention. The miraculous outcome was that Erik had a fully functional spleen (which is so critical for a developing youngster). This little boy recovered well from this serious and life-threatening injury.

There are many more stories about Erik and near catastrophes, but he made it to be a very able and fine young man. Erik is now an individual with exceptional grace and athletic ability. Erik also has tons of brain power which he uses to serve and help people. He has two very active sons (whom he now must help protect and preserve from their exuberant activities). It is a thing of beauty to see such a life saved for God's purposes. Erik's comment in retrospect was, "Even if I didn't volunteer for these events, God had a plan, and each event and interaction is purposeful in shaping us."

Jeremiah 29:11. "For I know the plans I have for you," declares the Lord, "plans to prosper you and not to harm you, plans to give you hope and a future."

Thank You, Lord, for preserving our lives when catastrophe strikes. In Jesus' name, Amen

Pay It Forward

It was 8:00 AM on a beautiful Saturday morning when the bicycling group met at their favorite starting point—a restaurant near a trail designated for walkers and bicyclists. The group of six cyclists rode about three miles and crossed Washington Avenue near West Virginia University Hospital in Wheeling, West Virginia. As they crossed this road, there was no traffic, and they all were keeping a good pace (maybe fifteen miles an hour).

Scott and Bill were leading the pack when Scott saw a stick on the path and called out a warning to the group. The stick (which was about one inch in diameter) may have been too near for Bill to avoid it, even though he acknowledged the warning. Bill hit the stick without slowing and his bicycle fork snapped in two on both sides, so that the handlebars were no longer attached securely. The bike tire lodged against the frame of the bicycle and stopped the wheel suddenly and completely, so that Bill flew over the front of the bike and landed on his helmet and face on the blacktop trail. Because of the speed of the bike and the sudden stop, it was a forceful fall. The impact went mainly into Bill's face, head, and neck.

Thankfully, Scott was trained in emergency medicine for his position in the coal mine where he was employed. He would not let anyone move Bill. He knew that his spine was likely fractured and should not be displaced.

Often, this group rides on country roads where there is no cell-phone reception, but this accident happened right in town where they had a good signal. Because of this and the accident location close to the hospital, the ambulance arrived very quickly.

Bill was unconscious after he hit the ground, and the first sound he heard afterwards was the ambulance siren. The ceiling of the hospital was the first thing that he saw as he was rolled down the hallway. As they wheeled him on a gurney over the door thresholds to take him from the Emergency Room to get a CT scan, the jarring caused pain at each bump. The hospital personnel told Bill that he had been in a bicycle accident, which he could not remember at all. When he did try to recall, he thought it happened out in the country on McGraw's Run, which is a dangerous road with many blind curves and bad road surfaces, that the group occasionally rides.

One of the guys in the bicycling group called June, Bill's wife, right after the accident. As she rushed to the hospital, she kept asking God over and over to "Please God, let him be fixable!"

The same day of the accident, Bill had plastic surgery for the damage to his face. His lips and eyebrows had gotten torn up, and a muscle under his nose was ripped. (Looking at him now, you cannot see that he had facial injuries at all.)

It turned out that an awesome doctor (Dr. M), who had recently come from West Virginia University Medical Center, was Bill's neurosurgeon / doctor-in-charge of his care. (Wheeling Hospital had recently been taken over by West Virginia University Medical Center.) Dr. M cared for Bill like he was his valued friend. He minimized the bumping over the thresholds that caused Bill so much pain by working on Bill right where he was, as much as possible. He refused to send Bill to Morgantown (the mothership of WVU Medical Center) to have the halo put on him—he put it on right in Wheeling.

This doc was capable, up-to-date, compassionate, and very skilled. He gave Bill and June information throughout the ordeal and seemed totally humble as June told him that she was praying for him.

The day after the accident they did the repairs to Bill's neck. He had shattered C1 and C2. They put a spacer between C5 and C6 and C6 and C7. A plate was put in to stabilize from C5 through C7. For all the damage to heal, they put a halo brace on to keep everything stable. This halo is worn around-the-clock. The ring (or halo) around the head is held in place by four screws into the skull. The ring is attached by four bars to a stiff, lightweight vest (lined with lambswool) that fits around the chest. The halo immobilizes the neck and spine so that it moves as one with the body to allow the spinal injury to heal. Bill will have to wear the halo brace for up to six months.

Here is a brief anatomy lesson to better understand Bill's injury and the magnitude of his miracle. There are seven cervical (neck) vertebrae. In the canal inside of the whole column of vertebrae runs the spinal cord from the brain downwards to the sacrum (tailbone). The spinal cord sends signals to the rest of the body through nerve roots that come out at each vertebra. These nerve roots go into large nerves then smaller ones that go all over the body. These nerves carry signals out and then sensory nerves conduct signals back to the spinal cord. The spinal cord carries information up to the brain to let it know what is going on all over the body. C1 or 'atlas' supports the base of the skull, and 'axis' is C2. The innervation from the cervical spinal cord nerve roots go to some very crucial things. C4 innervates the diaphragm—if there is damage to the spinal cord or nerve root above or at C4 then a person cannot breathe and dies. Injury to the nerve roots that go to the arm muscles are also in the neck—damage often leaves a person paralyzed as a quadriplegic (all four limbs no longer function). The further down you get in the spine with the harm then the lower in the limbs the subsequent weakness will be. If damage occurs to the spine, but the vertebrae are stabilized so that the bones don't press against or cut the spinal cord or nerve roots, then long-term loss might be avoided.

At first, it was not known what residual damage Bill would have. Traumatic brain injury with all its short-term and long-term effects? Paralysis? Weakness? Loss of range of motion? Organ function issues? All of these were possibilities. Would Bill have to live in chronic pain? Would this active man now be reduced to a very limited lifestyle? Here are the answers we have thus far: Bill's brain appears to be fine. Other than the period of being unconscious, his memories are intact. He still seems sharp and up to his previous speed in thinking. All four limbs are functional. As for range of motion in his neck and arms, time will tell. There will possibly be some loss, but perhaps not. After all, Bill is a walking, talking miracle!

At first, his bike group came to his house to hang out, however, Bill did not hole up and stay home. He has been out to friends' homes and to restaurants. This horrendous accident is not bringing his life to a screeching halt. Will he bicycle again? At first, he said an absolute "No!" That answer seems to be getting less emphatic with time. He is considering a three-wheel bike that is close to the ground and much more stable.

Bill is no stranger to suffering. In the past, he had a tractor accident that left him with multiple plates stabilizing bones. There is no question that this is one tough man who also has a very capable and resilient wife.

I asked Bill if he thought he had experienced a miracle and his answer was, "The doctor said it was a miracle, so I believe him."

Dr. M told Bill, after seeing the miraculous results of this accident, that he is supposed to be here for some reason. He told Bill to pay it forward. Bill is still pondering all of this. Why is he still alive? What is God's purpose for him? He is watching, listening, and waiting for opportunities to pay it forward.

What is Bill's definition of a miracle? "Something only God can do, like the parting of the Red Sea." Bill is a quiet and humble man—it is visibly difficult for him to be the center of attention and to be called a walking miracle. His uncomplaining attitude, his love of those around him, and his unfailing kindness are already paying it forward, but I will be watching this quiet man to see God's hand in his life.

Philippians 2:4, "Let each of you look not only to his own interests, but also to the interests of others."

Father, may each of us constantly look for how we can pay it forward. Please give us eyes to see and ears to hear. Help us to have tender hearts towards You and towards other people. In Jesus' name, Amen

A Double Miracle

My friend Samantha Robinson is a twin. When her mom was pregnant, their insurance did not cover ultrasounds.

Because there was only one audible heartbeat, the doctor thought she was having one large baby. For that reason, Sam's mom had no special prenatal care or anything whatsoever to help or protect her with what turned out to be a high-risk pregnancy and birth. The babies came three months early and big surprise: there were two babies instead of one! Sam and her sister each weighed two pounds, fifteen ounces. Because of their tiny size, they had to stay in the newborn intensive care unit for a month. Yet, miracle of miracles, these two extremely small and premature babies had no problems except needing to grow a bit.

The second miracle took place when Sam was twelve years old, a year before she would commit her life to Christ at summer camp. The incident occurred on the last day of summer vacation–right before sixth grade started. Sam and her friends were playing baseball using an aluminum bat. Sam's friend was up to bat, and Sam was standing back to await her turn. Sam was far enough back to be safe from a regular two-handed swing, but the friend surprisingly let go with one hand and swung in a super wide arc with a one-armed swing. The bat caught Sam in her temple. It was a hard hit.

Although Sam did not quite pass out, her vision blurred She saw bright white with dark around it. She went to tell her mom but was not able to form words well. There was a gushing wound on her temple gaping about three-quarter inch open.

Sam's mom called an ambulance, and once inside of it, a frightened Samantha asked the EMT if she would die. He told her that she would not, which was true. If you know about head injuries, you may know that there are often later consequences from the head trauma. I have known people with what seemed like minor head injuries who have had problems for the rest of their lives—headaches, problems with cognition, sleep difficulty, depression and so on.

Sam had a concussion, but God protected her. She has not had continuing effects from this incident. She has a bright, agile, and inquisitive mind, and she also has a perseverance in going after goals that you rarely see. There have been no cognition issues or other consequences from her head wound.

Did this incident in her young life, when she thought that she would die, prepare Sam to hear God's call to her? At that young age few of us realize that we are mortal. Did this event impress on Sam's heart the brevity of this life and the need for much more than what this world has to offer? God would soon become Sam's heavenly Father when she accepted His call on her life at summer camp the next summer-- He had plans for her.

My friendship with Sam is only a few years old. We had a Food Network event at our church, in which we all try to learn how to take the best care of our bodies (as well as our souls and spirits). At the end of the teaching session, we put out a sign-up list for accountability partners in eating well and caring for our bodies. Sam was the only one who signed up. Without even knowing how to do it, Sam and I became accountability partners. Through this, we have gotten to know and love each other.

Some traits that I grew to recognize in Sam were a very humble spirit, a teachable heart, and a gentle soul. Sam has the courage to go into uncharted territory, and I believe that she will have a big part in leading and equipping Christians.

More scary things have come up in Sam's life, but she is learning to trust that God has her back even when things don't go the way she wishes. Sam is not only teachable but is a teacher, and I await seeing the great plans that God has for her use in building the kingdom. She has the type of heart that leads by example and pulls people along just because they see God's hand at work in her life. It is a great privilege to be part of her life and to watch her grow.

Jeremiah 1:5a "Before I formed you in the womb, I knew you, and before you were born, I consecrated you."

Thank You, God for the miracles You do to keep us alive and well. Thank You for having plans for us. In Jesus' name, Amen

Blood Poisoning (McLaughlin family story)

The earliest miracle that I can remember took place when I was in third grade. God preserved my life even though at that time I was a non-believer. (While I attended church with my family, I had not yet heard and received the gospel message for my own.)

As a tomboy, I was very active—exploring woods, climbing trees, pushing through undergrowth, and living in nature in every way possible for a seven-year-old girl. As a result of this, I always had cuts, scrapes, and bruises, to which I paid no attention.

Somehow, I had gotten a hawthorn-bush thorn in my left hand and did not have the good sense to notice it or get my parents to look at it. Thankfully, it was warm weather, and I was wearing a sleeveless dress to school.

My teacher, Mrs. Ireland, noticed that I had a red streak going up my arm, almost to my shoulder. She called my mother and insisted that Mom leave work, come to school to get me, and take me to our family doctor. At that time, we had a doctor (Dr. Morgan) who made house calls, who knew us well, and who cared about us. He saw me immediately.

Dr. Morgan knew right away that I had blood-poisoning. The streak, signaling infection in my blood, was moving rapidly up the vein in my arm towards my heart. If it had reached another few inches carrying the sepsis to my heart, I would have died. Either Mrs. Ireland, my teacher, had some medical knowledge of what was going on, or the Holy Spirit clued her in. I personally believe the latter.

The solution to my problem was quite simple. The doctor found the thorn, pulled it out and had me soak my hand in hot Epsom Salts water. I could literally watch the red streak go back down towards my hand, like a thermometer being shaken down. It was quick—I returned to school the next day.

Others may not see this as a miracle. However, consider that our class was a baby-boomer classroom with thirtysix kids. Mrs. Ireland was totally on her own with no teacher's assistant. Furthermore, I was a very shy, quiet kid who basically hid in my seat. Even getting up to sharpen my pencil was total agony for me. Also, I had no pain or reason to call attention to my arm--it was not bothering me in any way.

It was a miracle that a busy teacher noticed a reticent kid's silent problem. It was God's intervention that Mrs. Ireland knew definitively that I needed emergency care. It was a miracle that the doc's response was so quick and effective. (Think of modern-day medical care with hours of waiting in an emergency room to get intervention. Also remember the current practice of trying antibiotic after antibiotic before arriving at effective treatment. This simple medical solution of using Epsom salts soaks preceded that time.)

God cares for us even before we have a relationship with Him. We all bask in His presence and love even before the Holy Spirit draws our hearts to Him. He tenderly watches over us.

Acts 17:28 "In Him we live and move and have our being."

Thank You, God, for caring for us. In Jesus' name, Amen

Our Timothy's Birth (McLaughlin family story)

Lee and I married in August of 1973, and my pregnancy with Tim, our firstborn, began in 1975. I was twenty-two years old with lots of immaturity as well as ignorance about being a mom. Despite my youth and lack of preparation, I wanted a baby. I mean-- I REALLY WANTED A BABY!

This desire was awakened in me on one spring day in May of 1975. I was driving back from a patient's home after doing a home-health physical therapy visit. As was typical, I navigated over narrow, winding, hilly, country roads. Rarely did I meet other cars on these skinny lanes, but when it happened, we would both have to move somewhat onto the berm to allow for comfortable passing.

Along that twisty, thin road, a car came in the other direction to pass by my car on the opposite side of the road. Automatically, I slowed way down and tried to time our passing so that it would not happen on the narrow one-lane bridge (over a culvert) that was coming up. I should have just completely stopped and let the other car pass by. It looked like he was waving me across the small bridge, but at the last moment he sped over it. I had the choice of hitting the other car or hitting the cement bridge pylon because his vehicle filled the one-lane bridge. I chose to hit the cement pylon, and the other driver sped off without even slowing down.

Our car was totaled, but I was unhurt, except for a sore neck and a cut on one knee. Here is the significant part. From the moment that I knew that I would crash, time slowed down, and my life literally passed before my eyes. I was not sure if these were my last few seconds on earth, and the thought that filled my head was, "I WANT A BABY!"

By the way, our solitary car was destroyed, and Lee's response was merely, "Are you okay?!" No recriminations. No lecture on my bad driving. Only total love, along with joy that I was not hurt.

Thankfully, Lee was happy to accommodate me in getting pregnant, even though he was still finishing his master's degree in Mechanical Engineering at West Virginia University, and we were dependent on my income. We lived in a twelve by sixty-foot mobile home that my parents owned at that time. It had two tiny bedrooms. In our small room, we had to crawl over the bed to get to the closet or dresser. In the second bedroom there was just enough room for a crib, a small dresser, plus a washer and dryer. Every square inch of that trailer was used to accommodate stuff—under the couch, under dressers, on shelves, etc. (During my pregnancy, I started nesting-organizing and reorganizing the stuff. I had been a major slob, and to everyone's amusement and sometimes dismay, this pregnancy permanently changed me into a neatnik.)

Throughout my time of carrying Tim, I continued to do physical therapy in my home-health job. Because of having morning sickness all day long, I carried a Tupperware bowl with a sealing lid on my visits. My patients and their families were sweet and patient with my vomiting episodes. Often, I would come in the door for the visit and bolt immediately to the bathroom. Many of the women that I saw gave me advice:

"Make sure you eat what you crave, or you will mark the baby!"

"Pay close attention to your dreams. The baby can tell you what he needs through them."

These kind ladies would also regularly ply me with homemade or homegrown food. Some of the homes that I visited were farms, so I got produce. One time I was sent home with T-bone steaks from one of the cows that was butchered.

We accepted all these things with open arms because we were poor. Our idea of a big night out was to go to the Student Union and watch the free movie. Our luxury food was whatever was on sale at the store (a pound of hamburger was less than a dollar at that time). In those days working as a physical therapist did not pay well unless you had a private practice. Lee had a part-time job at the library in addition to his classes in graduate school. Despite our extreme conservation of money and resources, we ran out of food before each new payday. Then, we would 'happen' to show up at my parent's house, where they would stuff our tummies with food, fill our hearts with love, then send us home with leftovers.

If I was near Mom and Dad's house at noon, Mom and I would meet for lunch there, so she could feed me. I craved oranges so she always had a bag on-hand

The time finally arrived for Tim's arrival. My water broke with a gush on March 10, 1976, at about six in the morning. Concurrent with my amniotic fluid leak, the faucet on the bathtub started spurting water. Lee had to take care of that before we headed to the hospital. Lee and I thought it was hilarious that my water and the trailer's water broke at the same time.

Finally, our baby was on the way, and I was both excited and terrified. Lee and I had gone through natural childbirth classes. Apparently, Lee had not learned much from these because his idea of coaching was to eat Snickers bars and thump my feet when he thought I was not relaxing enough through my contractions. (If I had not been busy trying to give birth, he would have been a dead man.)

After informing the doctor again about my decision not to have drugs, my labor began in earnest, and everything seemed hunky-dory. There were regular contractions, about five minutes apart. In my naïveté and total ignorance, I told the doctor, "I don't know what all the fuss is about, this is like falling off a log."

To the doc's credit, if he fell over laughing, he waited until he was out of the room and beyond earshot. At 1:00 am the next morning, after seventeen-plus, long hours of hard labor, I had one long continuous contraction that seemed to go on for hours. The baby was in distress, and I was screaming, "Give me drugs!! Give me anything!!" It was not like falling off a log anymore.

I had an emergency Caesarian-section, and our poor Tim had a cone-shaped head from the pounding he received. He had been battered against my pelvis, instead of going through the birth canal.

Tim was born at 2:20 am, and both of us were totally worn out by the ordeal of childbirth. The nurses insisted that I go to sleep and would not give him to me. However, I was infinitely more stubborn than they were. Finally, the nurse gave up and put Tim on my chest. Our beautiful boy raised his head and looked right into my eyes. It was pure love at first sight.

Despite all he had been through, Tim was a robust, good sized baby, however they put him in an incubator because that was routine for a C-section baby. Tim was so active that every few minutes the nurses would have to adjust his position in the incubator because he would stick an arm or leg through the access holes meant for the nurse's arms. He regularly woke all the babies in the nursery with his hungry crying when it was time to come to Mom and nurse once again. Always, he led the baby-brigade to the moms. (We should have seen then that he would be a natural leader.)

Timothy means "honoring God". This little guy had quite a name to grow into. Here are the apostle Paul's instructions to his protégé, Timothy, in the Bible.

Timothy 4:11-16 "Command and teach these things. Let no one despise you for your youth, but set the believers an example in speech, in conduct, in love, in faith, in purity. Until I come, devote yourself to the public reading of Scripture, to exhortation, to teaching. Do not neglect the gift you have, which was given you by prophecy when the council of elders laid their hands on you. Practice these things, immerse yourself in them, so that all may see your progress. Keep a close watch on yourself and on the teaching. Persist in this, for by so doing you will save both yourself and your hearers."

Our beautiful son! Such a huge miracle—thank You Lord! In Jesus' name, Amen

Our Kevin's Birth (McLaughlin family story)

My pregnancy with our youngest son, started in 1980. We were wanting to have a baby, but before we knew that I was pregnant—I got a major case of poison ivy and took some prescribed corticosteroids to help with the itching and swelling. When we found out that I was pregnant, we were thrilled but concerned about effects from the medicine.

That was just the beginning of our worries. I was working (doing home health physical therapy) during my pregnancy, and I was exposed to active tuberculosis with one of my patients in my early pregnancy. Also, for the first portion of my pregnancy I had morning sickness all day, to the point that I could not keep anything down. This ended in ketonuria, which can cause neurological damage in the baby. (Ketones in my urine meant that I was breaking down my body's fat because of lack of nutrition, and this put high levels of ketones into my body and possibly into our baby's body also.) Because of this, my doctor put me in the hospital to get intravenous nutrition. Then, I got a viral bug that put me in the hospital once again—I had a fever of 104 degrees. The doctor told me that whatever my temperature was, the baby's temp was one to two degrees higher. All these things could harm our baby in various ways, from damaging his brain to causing birth defects. We were anxious, and our doctor was also worried.

We were still living in Point Marion, Pennsylvania, and we had recruited many to pray for our baby's health. An amazing thing happened--people whom we did not even know were praying. We would go to the grocery store, and when we would write a check, the cashier would see our name and say, "We are praying for your baby." At the bank, a similar thing occurred. Our church family was praying, and our family's churches were praying. People came out of the woodwork to tell us they were praying for a healthy baby.

Still, I was nervous. So was the doctor—she watched the baby and me like a hawk.

The third trimester got better. As the pregnancy progressed, I made up for lost time with eating. I could and did keep my food down. The baby got bigger, and I became huge, gaining forty pounds total.

The time finally arrived for Kevin to come, but nothing happened. No Braxton-Hicks contractions. No hint whatsoever that our baby planned to exit the uterus. I told the doctor that I was sure that he was completely baked, but he was just comfy, cozy, and happy in the womb. Nevertheless, she wanted to wait longer to schedule the C-section.

Finally, on March 9, 1981, the surgery was scheduled. (We chose to have a different day than Tim's birthday on March 10 so that they each would have separate birthdays.) I was put in a room to wait on the start-up procedures for the surgery. Alone. All by myself. Just me.

All my concerns started to surface, and my anxiety skyrocketed. I picked up the Gideon's Bible that was in the room and started randomly opening it. Here are the three stories that I opened to, one after the other-- just by opening the Bible three times in a row:

Luke 8: 43-48. "And a woman was there who had been subject to bleeding for twelve years, but no one could heal her. She came up behind him and touched the edge of his cloak, and immediately her bleeding stopped. "Who touched me?" Jesus asked. When they all denied it, Peter said, "Master, the people are crowding and pressing against you." But Jesus said, "Someone touched me; I know that power has gone out from me." Then the woman, seeing that she could not go unnoticed, came trembling and fell at his feet. In the presence of all the people, she told why she had touched him and how she had been instantly healed. Then he said to her, "Daughter, your faith has healed you. Go in peace."

Luke 7:1-10 "After he had finished all his sayings in the hearing of the people, he entered Capernaum. Now a centurion had a servant who was sick and at the point of death, who was highly valued by him. When the centurion heard about Jesus, he sent to him elders of the Jews, asking him to come and heal his servant. And when they came to Jesus, they pleaded with him earnestly, saying, "He is worthy to have you do this for him, for he loves our nation, and he is the one who built us our synagogue." And Jesus went with them. When he was not far from the house, the centurion sent friends, saying to him, "Lord, do not trouble yourself, for I am not worthy to have you come under my roof. Therefore, I did not presume to come to you. But say the word, and let my servant be healed. For I too am a man set under authority, with soldiers under me: and I say to one, 'Go,' and he goes; and to another, 'Come,' and he comes; and to my servant, 'Do this,' and he does it." When Jesus heard these things, he marveled at him, and turning to the crowd that followed him, said, "I tell you, not even in Israel have I found such faith." And when those who had been sent returned to the house, they found the servant well." And:

Matthew 15: 21-27 "Leaving that place, Jesus withdrew to the region of Tyre and Sidon. A Canaanite woman from that vicinity came to Him, crying out, "Lord, Son of David, have mercy on me! My daughter is suffering terribly from demon-possession."

Jesus did not answer a word. So, his disciples came to Him and urged Him, "Send her away, for she keeps crying out after us." He answered, "I was only sent to the lost sheep of Israel."

The woman came and knelt before Him. "Lord, help me!" she said. He replied, "It is not right to take the children's bread and toss it to their dogs." "Yes, Lord," she said, "but even the dogs eat the crumbs that fall from their master's table." Then Jesus answered, "Woman, you have great faith! Your request is granted." And her daughter was healed from that very hour."

Finally, I got the message. 'God is in charge. Trust him.
Have faith in him.' I chose to do just that and trust God no
matter what happened.

The surgery went well. Kevin was delivered in the late
afternoon. He was a big baby—ten pounds even. The
doctor said, "Why don't we just let him walk right out of
here?"

There was absolutely nothing wrong with him. The doctors
were convinced that there had to be a health problem, so
they kept trying to find one. He was completely one-
hundred percent healthy.

Baby Kevin was chill-- so relaxed and contented. We had
chosen the name Stephen, but after we met our baby, we
decided on Kevin.

The Greek meaning of Kevin means "gentle and kind".

Colossians 3:12. Therefore, as God's chosen people, holy
and dearly loved, clothe yourselves with compassion,
kindness, humility, gentleness, and patience.

Matthew 17: 20b. … Truly I tell you, if you have faith as
small as a mustard seed, you can say to this mountain,
'Move from here to there,' and it will move. Nothing will
be impossible for you."

Thank You, Lord, for another wonderful miracle and the
gift of our third beautiful boy! In Jesus' name, Amen

Kevin and Space Mountain (McLaughlin family story)

When the boys were young, we took a few trips to
Disneyworld in Florida. Lee, with his engineering
knowledge, refused to go on the rides, so I was the adult to
accompany our sons on all the attractions. (In retrospect,
Lee may have been the wise one.)

On our last trip, Kevin, our youngest, finally had enough height to be allowed on more than the little-kid rides. He had always been too short to go on the wild Space Mountain roller-coaster attraction, and this was a desire of his heart. On our last family Disneyworld trip, he was finally tall enough, so he and I went on his long-awaited Space Mountain jaunt.

We put Kevin on the side that would push him into me, instead of centrifugal force smashing my mass into him. The high school (or college age) kid came along and shut the bar and checked it (maybe not very well). There were no additional seat belts. We were ready to go.

Off we sped into our first curve and jostle. To my huge dismay, the bar that kept us locked in place popped open, so we were no longer held into the car. Thankfully, I had my arm around Kev already. Leaning toward him, I put the other arm around him and held on for dear life. He was small so he bounced a lot, and it seemed beyond my capability to hold him in the car. I prayed my very theological, deep, and well-thought-out plea to God (sarcasm). "JESUS HELP!!!" The ride seemed interminable to me. I never talked or even looked at Kevin's face because I was so intent on keeping him from flying out.

When the ride finally ended, I unlocked my sore arms and hands from their death grip on Kevin. All the muscles and joints in my body were aching and burning. I looked at Kev, expecting that he would be totally terrorized. He was smiling from ear to ear, and he was ready to do it again. Apparently, he thought that was what adult rides were like. He had a blast!

Psalm 121:7-8 "The Lord keeps you from all harm and watches over your life. The Lord keeps watch over you as you come and go, both now and forever."

Thank You, God, for the strength you gave me to hold on to Kevin. Thanks for preserving his life and keeping him from being traumatized by our danger. In Jesus' name, Amen

Kevin and the Seatbelt (McLaughlin family story)

When Kevin was in his junior year of high school, he and two buddies decided to skip school for a day. (I did not learn the truancy part of the story until decades later. In the version Kev told me then, they just went out for lunch.) During that period (around 1998), it was easier for kids to ditch school undetected. School officials did not utilize the electronic means that they do now to know where kids are at any given time.) On that day, there was a field trip planned to see the movie, 'Schindler's List' and to hear a holocaust survivor speak of his experiences. These three boys figured they would not be missed on the field trip, and they were right.

One of Kev's friends, Matt, was driving on their outing. Another friend was in the passenger seat, and Kev was in the back seat. Usually, when sitting in the back seat, Kevin did not put on his seat belt. (At that time, in Illinois, it was not required by law.) However, on this day, Kevin felt the inner nudge to buckle his seat belt. That action may have saved his life or at least prevented a much greater injury.

The three guys were traveling through our township, Libertyville, on a four-lane, busy highway. Matt started fooling with the audio system while he was driving, trying to put a CD in the player. Unexpectedly, traffic came to a stop in front of them. Matt was going about thirty-five miles per hour when he slammed into the back of the car that stopped in front of him. None of the three boys ended up with serious injuries, thanks to their seatbelts.

Nonetheless, there were consequences because of their choice to skip school. Matt's car was totaled. Kevin ended up aggravating a previous sternum hairline-fracture that he had from a soccer injury. Plus, these three guys missed out on a once-in-a lifetime chance to hear and learn from a holocaust survivor. God's protection and the quiet miracle came in the gentle whisper telling Kev to put on his seat belt.

Romans 8:14" For those who are led by the Spirit of God are the children of God."

Thank You, God for protecting Kevin. Thanks for leading him to buckle his seat belt. Thank You also that throughout the course of his life Kevin has learned to hear You, obey You, and to love You more and more. In Jesus' name, Amen

Patrick's Fall (McLaughlin family story)

When Patrick and Kevin were at Clemson University, they made it a practice to go to a nearby lake and swim. At their favorite place on the lake, there was a rope swing tied to a big tree. None of us knew how dangerous this swing would turn out to be.

About two weeks before the incident happened, I had a dream. It was one of my few dreams that I knew was a communication from God. In the wee hours of the morning, I awakened-- trembling, and crying-- from a very realistic dream in which Patrick was being carried in a coffin by Lee and Kevin.

Lee and I took it as a warning to pray for Patrick's protection. We began entreating God for Patrick's safety, as constantly as was humanly possible, from the time of the dream until the accident happened. Moreover, I called my friends, Gail, and Ivy, early the next morning after having the dream. I knew they would take the warning seriously, and I knew absolutely, without a doubt, that they would also call out to God diligently.

So, we all prayed and waited. I thought something would happen quickly, but it did not. Then, the call came about two weeks later from Kevin about Patrick—he was at the local hospital near Clemson.

Patrick, Kevin, and a friend of theirs had gone to the lake. They were taking turns swinging on the rope-swing out over the lake then dropping into the water. On one of Patrick's turns, the rope caught against the trunk of the tree instead of swinging freely. It stopped the rope-swing arc abruptly and roughly shook Patrick off, not over the water, but rather over big, jagged rocks on the very steep hillside.

It was a precipitous slope and a long fall. Kevin and his friend saw the height of Patrick's fall onto the sharp stones, and both thought that Patrick was dead on impact. Kevin called 911, but the emergency workers could not reach Patrick from the steeply angled hillside. They had to send in a boat to take him by water to the waiting ambulance.

Kevin eventually managed to climb down to Patrick. He saw that Patrick was alive but was in absolute agony. Patrick's head was badly beaten up from the fall, and his chest had also hit the rocks and had large areas of discoloration. When the emergency workers arrived, they were making Patrick's pain even worse as they tried to put him on a stretcher.

While seeing the extent of Patrick's pain, Kevin was crying and praying at the same time. At one point, when Patrick's pain seemed unbearable, Kev pushed the workers' hands back so that he could touch Patrick and pray for him. He felt like something happened (in a good way) as he prayed.

The EMT's then took Patrick off in the boat. Patrick later said it was an extremely terrifying experience because he was tightly strapped on the stretcher on a fast-moving boat, and it felt like he could slide right over the edge into the water.

Meanwhile, Kevin made it to the hospital in his car and called us. The doctors immediately began doing various tests on Patrick to see how much damage was done. They seemed pretty sure that he would have organ damage. Also, they were concerned about bleeding inside his skull from the impact to his head.

Patrick's nurse began communicating with us long distance by phone. She talked to me 'Mom to Mom'. She said that she had kids and she would give me the straight dope. As the tests came in, the only thing that showed up was some bad bruising. No broken bones, no skull or brain injury, no internal bleeding, and no organ damage.

Lee and I were scrambling to get a plane flight down to Clemson—we were going to have to go a-round-about way with lots of connecting flights because there were no last-minute direct flights available. After all the tests and exams, the nurse told us not to come--Patrick was fine. He would not look pretty for a while with his black eyes, swelling, and dark bruises, but God had protected him.

2 Samuel 22:3 "My God is my rock, in whom I take refuge, my shield and the horn of my salvation."

Thank You, Father, for preserving Patrick's life. Thanks for giving us the warning to pray and for letting us see the miracle and work of Your loving hands. In Jesus' name, Amen

Lawn Mowing (McLaughlin family story)

We own thirty acres of West Virginia hill country, and we mow about two of those with lawn mowers. Because I love to do the areas that can be done on the riding-mower; this has been my job from the point of acquiring this property. There is one portion which we used to mow which is steeper than everywhere else. We no longer mow it, and you will soon understand why. That sharply angled slope was the area that I mowed on the day of my misadventure.

When I started cutting our lawn after we bought our farm, I knew nothing about riding mower safety. Lee's dad taught me how to mow with a tractor on hillsides. You don't go across the slopes—instead you go straight up the slope and straight down. However, even with safe techniques, a couple of things can make mowing less stable. Hitting an unexpected hole and having moisture on the grass are two of those things.

On the day when I was mowing, I had the perfect storm of these conditions in addition to the precipitous terrain. As I said previously, the portion that I was cutting was the steepest part of all the area that we kept mown. It was mid-morning in the heat of summer when the dew is usually dry, and I was on our John Deere riding mower. It turned out that on this shady hillside there was still some moisture. Also, as I was going downhill on the damp grass, I hit a hidden groundhog hole.

Our lawn tractor spun around and flipped me completely off the seat. The engine is supposed to immediately turn off when you are unseated. However, this cut-off mechanism took long enough to stop so that when I fell and my foot slipped under the mower deck, the mower blade was still turning. It cut into my tennis shoe and chewed the end of it completely off, right up to where my toes filled the sneaker.

Other that being completely shaken up, I was unhurt. All my toes were intact. My shoe was destroyed exactly to the point where my toes started and no further. I kept that shoe for quite a while to remind me of how God loves and protects us.

Psalm 34:7-9 "For the angel of the Lord is a guard; he surrounds and defends all who fear him. Taste and see that the Lord is good. Oh, the joys of those who take refuge in him! Fear the Lord, you his godly people, for those who fear him will have all they need."

Another miracle! Thanks to our merciful and loving God. In Jesus' name, Amen

Close Encounter with a Wheel (McLaughlin family story)

This event happened when our boys were still living at home with us. They were strong and able-bodied teens and willing to be free labor, especially for their beloved granddad. Lee's dad had an old barn on his property that had been used for storage. As most storage-type facilities do, this building had collected lots of stuff through the years--almost all of it was dirty, rusty junk, with mice nests and droppings mixed throughout. Grandpa requested that we bring our built-in family labor force for a visit to help him 'de-junkify' his old barn.

Our whole family made the trip to Wheeling, West Virginia, from our Chicago home. We planned the excursion to do double duty—to get in a visit with Lee's parents and sisters, plus to clean the barn. On a gorgeous, sunny, summer Saturday, Lee's father (Lee Senior), Lee, and the three boys trekked the country path to the barn and set to work. Lee's mom and his sisters had gone to a baby shower. (You will see why this is pertinent in a minute.) Lee Senior was directing the clean-up—the guys were sorting into a burning, trash, give-away, and keep piles. It was a challenging job—lots of heat, dust, and filth. I was observing and occasionally carrying a light item here or there. Things were moving along quite well and quickly.

I took a break and went back to the house, which was about a quarter-mile walk. About that time, Lee's mom and sisters returned from their party. They asked about where all the guys were, and I told them what the males of our family were doing.

What happened next was totally unexpected. Lee's sisters were quite upset, even tearful, at the idea of the barn being cleared out. Apparently, the barn had always been off limits to them. They were not sure what stored treasures of theirs were in there, and it bothered them greatly that they had not even had a chance to check things over before they were possibly thrown away. At the time, I did not understand their reaction because I had seen how mouse-eaten, mildewed, and filthy everything was. (Now, I do understand—it was an emotional response because of some childhood taboos and restrictions that were typical for females in that period.) I carried the message up to Lee, his dad, and our sons. They stopped their work, put stuff back, and closed the barn.

Meanwhile, I was very upset after the encounter with the girls. Understand, that I am a burden-bearer. That means that I perceive things from other people's spirits and take on those feelings into my own spirit. After sensing the intense anguish from Lee's sisters, I needed some space and time by myself. I asked Lee's dad if I could borrow their little red Dodge Colt to drive to Morgantown to spend time with my parents (the Colt was a tiny car that was easy to drive). Lee Senior said yes, of course I could use his car.

I took the interstate and was tooling along in the little vehicle. Traffic was heavy, with both lanes filled. I was behind a newer looking panel truck. Fortunately, I was about three to four car lengths back from him. Furthermore, because I needed God's comfort, I had been praying the whole time since I left the driveway.

The next thing that happened was crazy. The right rear wheel (not just the tire) came completely off the axle of the panel truck in front of me and started rolling directly towards my car. I could not go onto the berm because the panel truck was pulling over there. (He managed to control his van while his axle was scraping on the road making horrible screeching noises and shooting sparks everywhere. His ability to control the car was a miracle in itself!) Furthermore, I could not go into the left lane because there was a car next to me in that lane and a car in front of that car. The lane, in which I was currently driving, was blocked by the wheel rolling in its straight path directly towards me.

Did I mention that I had been praying the whole drive? That is important—the instantaneous call for help might not have been as easy for me to transition into, if I were not already in praying mode. Just like my accident in my early twenties', everything turned into slow motion. The wheel coming at me was on a collision course with the right front of my car. I slowed as much as possible but could not slam on my brakes because of traffic behind me.

As I prayed and watched, the wheel from the van turned ninety degrees and headed harmlessly off towards the berm. What would have been a multi-car, disastrous accident was completely averted. Still praying, I drove shakily on towards my parents' house. My prayers now had completely changed to giving thanks. Never had I seen such a complete, quick, and obvious intervention! A miracle from a loving Father.

Job 1:10 "You have always put a wall of protection around him and his home and his property."

Father, thank You for Your tender care. Thank You for putting a hedge of protection around us. In Jesus' name, Amen

A Big Wreck (McLaughlin family story)

When we lived in a suburb outside of Chicago, we would often get massive snowfalls. Because this was typical weather for our area, the snowplows would clear the roads quickly and make them passable.

One such winter morning after about six inches of snow had fallen, I chose to run some errands because the roads were already cleared off. However, because I am a naturally cautious person, I was driving slowly (maybe twenty-five to thirty miles per hour) southwards on a fourlane highway that went North-South between two townships. I was in the left lane because my destination was coming up on that side. A large black SUV was beside me in the right lane—it was traveling at a speed higher than mine (maybe forty mph, which was the speed limit in that section of road). It did feel to me like he was going faster than he should have been in the snowy weather.

The roads in our township were perfectly clear, and the black SUV had no problems until he reached the border for the next township. There, the roads had not been cleared, and his speed was too high for the snowy conditions he encountered. I saw what was happening and hit the brakes, but his vehicle hit the snow, spun completely around, and ended up in my lane with the driver right in the line of impact from my car.

Here comes the miracle. This was a four-lane, busy highway, and there were cars in all the lanes, including the ones on the opposite side going north. There was piled up snow in the median and on both sides of the road.

I did not want to run directly into the guy driving the SUV, so I veered left, hit, and bounced off the front end of his car. The impact caused me to veer farther left across the median then through the two lanes of heavy northbound traffic. My car ended up in a snowbank on the other side of the four-lane road. The speed of his car plus the impact of his vehicle against mine added to the velocity that I was traveling. Yet despite my speed and notwithstanding the heavy traffic, my car reached the other side of the road (into the piled-up snowbank) without striking another vehicle. All the north-bound cars managed to completely navigate around my car without hitting me as I crossed those lanes. There were no further wrecks on that crowded highway caused by the chain of events in this accident.

God protected me and the driver of the black SUV. He was completely unhurt, as was I. This time I did not even have a sore neck or a scrape.

1 Peter 5:7 "Cast all your anxiety on him because he cares for you."

Thank You, Lord, for your protection everywhere. In Jesus' name, Amen

Conclusions

Looking for patterns and for ways to help bring about these miracles of protection left me feeling clueless. Some of these events involved God reaching down without any apparent prayer being raised up to ask for help, like the protection of Samantha and Angela. Then, there were those where prayer was a constant outcry for God's intervention like Karen praying for her son and Bob and Bill praying for a rescue in the cave.

There is obviously not a monopoly by Christians in being protected by God. Sam was not yet a Christian when born three months premature and when she had protection during her head injury. Likewise, I was not a Christian when saved from the blood poisoning.

It seems like God answers prayers but also just pours out His mercy at times. Can we be part of prayers of protection? It seems to me that every Christian parent would say yes: pray for God to watch over your loved ones.

However, God is merciful. Many times, He protects us, and we don't even notice or tell Him thank you. My heart's response to these miracles is to be thankful that we have a caring Lord. Also, we need to be looking for the happenings when God watches over us so that we can give Him the thanks and praise so deserved.

Questions to ponder:

1. Have you thought about the many times that God has protected you?
2. Can you share some of your stories?
3. Have you expressed your gratitude to God?

CHAPTER 3--MIRACLES OF HEALING

We do get sick, have injuries, and have bad things happen in our lives. Yet, our God is involved and intervening. He is not a watchmaker-God who started it all then sits back to observe—our Father God loves us and cares about each detail in our lives.

Here are a lot of healing stories which are not always easy to hear. These people went through some hard times but came out knowing more deeply the enormity of God's love through both the good and the bad.

Healing with Unconditional Love

Upon hearing this heartbreaking account of two people who were abused as children, I wondered how many of the later consequences in their lives resulted from their early exploitation. Yet, if you currently encountered Seth and Carol (not their real names), you would say, "No way they were abused, they are both so remarkably whole and outrageously joyful. They could not have come from such a damaging background." Yet, both survived horrific events. Seth was repeatedly sexually abused (over a period of approximately a year) by an older neighborhood boy when he was eight years old. Carol was sexually abused by her older brother, in almost-nightly assaults that lasted for a long period.

This is not something that either of them wears on their sleeves--neither is it something that they choose to hide. Several years ago, Carol used her experience and recovery to teach young girls that they have a right to say no with the 'True Love Waits' program. Seth has participated in groups in Alcoholics Anonymous and other rehab programs specifically addressing sexual abuse of boys. His transparency has doubtlessly helped to heal many boys and men with similar backgrounds of mistreatment.

Stemming from the desire to begin the healing work that needed to happen and fueled by the determination that the abuse would not have any victorious power in their marriage bed, Carol made a critical decision. She knew that she had to tell Seth, the most important person in her life, what had happened to her as a child. Her incapacity to love herself (because of her wounds) and the realization of other behaviors that were born out of the abuse became more evident to her. She shared her story with her minister and then asked if he would join her when she revealed it to Seth. Carol was afraid that he might react in destructive anger and possibly violence without a calming presence. She knew that in the moment of being told, Seth's relationship with her brother could radically change from that of a close friend to one with a person who had cruelly and selfishly wounded his wife.

There was one additional scenario that was a large part in the unfurling dynamics. At that time, Carol's brother had been married to Seth's sister for five years, and their marriage was rapidly deteriorating, soon to end in a divorce. A not so small miracle was that Carol and Seth would have never met without the marriage of their siblings. As Seth and Carol approach being married for forty-five years, they pause to reflect that perhaps the

Lord was at that time orchestrating a bigger plan for the two of them.

Continuing with Seth's story, at thirteen years old he began drinking alcohol and using drugs (mostly pain killers and marijuana, along with occasional trials of other drugs). His justification to himself was that he needed relief for the pain from football injuries. From seventh grade onward, Seth played defensive positions, like linebacker, and his knees were badly banged up. These injuries continued to escalate—in his sophomore year in high school, Seth tore the cartilage in his left knee and in his junior year he did the same to his right knee. Physical pain became his constant companion from an early age. (To understand the depth of his suffering, know that Seth had to have both knees replaced as a relatively young man.)

As an extremely high functioning addict, Seth never missed school or work. Nevertheless, to get pain relief or a high from alcohol and drugs, Seth kept increasing the amounts that he used. This pattern continued until October 31, 1988, (Halloween) when Seth was thirty-three years old.

Seth was at work on that autumn day and discovered that he was completely out of pills. He had never let this happen before, but on this day, Seth could not seem to get his mind to work like normal. He was agitated, walking in and out of his office. Seth was trying unsuccessfully to remember where he had gotten his last prescription filled. (He routinely alternated his prescription purchases between different drug stores to keep them from suspecting the large number of pills he consumed.) In his restless wanderings on that day of crisis, Seth ended up in the workplace restroom. Out in the outer office his coworkers heard a thud, which sounded something like a file cabinet falling over. When Seth was discovered passed out on the bathroom floor, they quickly called 911.

The paramedics arrived and began questioning Seth (who was now conscious and seated at his desk after his first grand mal seizure). "Did he know his name, where he was, the current date, and his birthdate?" His responses were all "No's" until they reached this question, "Are you taking any drugs that we should know about?" Seth said "Yes" to this query.

It was then that God spoke to Seth in an audible voice as clearly as if he were right there next to him. The Lord's saving voice said "It's all over. You're going to be okay." This was a pivotal moment in Seth's life--it was the very last day of his substance abuse. At that instant, Seth's need for drugs and alcohol stopped, and that desire has never returned to this day.

Seth had another grand mal seizure in the ambulance and again at the hospital--the drug and alcohol use had taken a heavy toll on his body. He was thereafter transported from the emergency room to a local ten-day detox program. This was followed directly with a thirty-day inpatient drug and alcohol rehab program. Although Seth's desire for substances was gone, he wanted to participate in all the therapies and education that were offered to him. After rehab, he complied with the treatment plan of attending ninety Alcoholics Anonymous meetings in ninety days and secured a sponsor within the group. His commitment took him to AA meetings for the next fifteen years and to date he celebrates thirty-three years of sobriety.

At the rehab facility, Seth was part of a small group with a skilled therapist and some of the other patients. The therapist would focus on one person at a time, spending the first two weeks tearing them down (with the goal of helping them see the roots of their addictions), and then the last two weeks were spent building them back up. Seth had only mentioned his past sexual abuse in one of the group meetings, but no in-depth discussion of the matter had occurred. One day, the therapist deliberately moved Seth's opportunity to tell his story to the end of the session. After he had shared his story with the group, the therapist instructed Seth to write a letter to his abuser and to bring it with him the following day.

Seth worked hard on that letter, pouring out both the anger and anguish that had been stored inside of him for twenty five years. (His abuser had previously died by suicide, so confrontation or legal proceedings were not possible.) At the meeting the next day, Seth read his letter aloud to the group. His therapist then instructed him to hold the letter with both hands, pulling it apart as hard as he could, just short of tearing it. At the same time, he was asked to yell out all the rage and pain that had lived inside of him for so long. Repeated screams came from deep within him. These resounded beyond the walls of the room and left Seth without a voice. With that symbolic bodily action, an obvious peace began to take residence in Seth, and he started to forgive and heal. He grew to understand that he could no longer bury, drown, or bypass his emotional pain…it was necessary to call upon God's help as he plowed straight through the hurt.

Although Carol had shared her history of sexual abuse with Seth early-on in their marriage, Seth had repressed his. After writing the letter, he knew that Carol had to hear his story. He telephoned her and asked if she could come for a visit on the weekend. His voice was very hoarse after his soul-rending screams of pain, and somehow Carol knew that whatever Seth needed to say was serious. With trepidation, Carol made the trip to see Seth, wondering if their marriage was in jeopardy. After Seth shared, she looked at him and said, "Aren't we just like two peas in a pod?" Over the subsequent years as health issues and a range of life-hurdles presented, they would both lean into God and know he was giving them 'more glue for their tube' to restore their wholeness. They used all the various trials to strengthen their trust in God and their love for one another.

Carol had already worked hard at her own healing with the help of therapists and her pastor. Instead of going the path of drugs and alcohol in response to her wounds, Carol had built defenses by overachieving (while underneath all the competence, she was insecure and needing unconditional love). Through counseling, prayer, and the outpouring of over-the-top love from many people, (especially Seth and her friend Julie), Carol was greatly healed. However, that day of conversation with Seth at the rehab facility showed her something that she lacked--peace. Seth now had a peace surpassing understanding that Carol wanted. The beginning of opening the door to that peace took Carol to the same facility where Seth had been. This was a one-week inpatient program, designed for any family member of the patients who had successfully completed their thirty-day program. She also did some hard work with a therapist and a small group dealing with how her sexual abuse had impacted her life. So much of her personality had been shaped by her past. The door had "cracked open" and Carol was hungry for the peace and joy that she knew could only come from God.

Both Carol and Seth were determined to keep their marriage bed undefiled by memories. Before intimate moments, Seth would ask for the Lord to keep their minds and hearts pure. Talking to God became such a part of Seth's existence that praying simultaneously to life's happenings became second nature. Carol also became a person of profound communication with God—a Bible study / prayer group at their church was crucial in learning how to go deeper with God.

Seth went on occasional weekends away with men from his AA 'home group'. One of the men who knew Seth's story, mentioned he had seen an ad in the paper about an eight-week program designed to help men who had been sexually abused. Seth realized this would be entirely different from his experience at the rehab center. This time would give him the opportunity to interact with other men who could directly relate to the scars the abuse had left on him. In sharing his story again and in listening to other stories like his, more tears flowed in the cleansing of his mind and heart.

The healing process continued with both seeking counseling, prayer, and unconditional love from God and others around them. Carol reached the point that she knew her parents (now divorced) must also know the truth about the abuse. Carol's dad, who once was an angry and violent man, had changed to being tenderhearted when Carol was eighteen years old. At the age of twenty-four, Carol told her father about the abuse and was immediately engulfed in his love and grief for what she had gone through. He regretted not being a better protector--many times over the ensuing years Carol's dad tearfully and genuinely asked for her forgiveness, which she freely gave.

When Carol was ready to share with her mom (an active alcoholic), she knew she would need extra support present at the meeting. Her therapist had prepared her, in that she needed to be ready for a variety of responses. One of these could be that her mother would not believe her. To give her support, she took Seth, her therapist, and their minister to the meeting. When told, her mother asked her why Carol had not come to her when the abuse started. Without allowing Carol time to answer, she quickly interjected, "If I had known, the roof would have blown off our house." Carol knew from a young age that both of her parents had volatile tempers, and she had feared a violent reaction in the telling, especially from her father. She had witnessed her father push her mother down a set of stairs, breaking her arm in the process. This was just one of the constant verbal and physical fights between her parents. SILENCE seemed to be the only option that she had to keep her family intact. This was her first lesson in the creed of 'peace at any price.' Moreover, the 1960's was a period that was in stark contrast to all the prevention tools and campaigns that now exist in the family and school community. She knew of no safe place where she could voice that "someone was touching her in the wrong places."

After the meeting with Carol's mother, they returned home, where Carol's mom shared for the first time, that she had been sexually abused by her father. Thinking this revelation may have given her mom a greater level of insight or empathy did not prove to be true. As the years passed, Carol's mother seemed to sweep the whole matter under the rug, therein illustrating the power denial has in an alcoholic's life.

During the assaults, Carol used one of the most powerful defense mechanisms that people use in a traumatic event-

disassociation. In her mind, she was able to escape by mentally separating herself from the young girl laying on the bed. The best description was 'as if her soul left her body and hovered over the bed'. This allowed her to separate and distance herself from the reality of what was being forced upon her.

As one of the final steps in Carol's healing, she had an impulse to revisit the house where the abuse took place. The home belonged to another family by that time. The place she lingered the longest was on the threshold of her bedroom door. There, she allowed her adult self to spend time feeling all the emotions that had been frozen inside of her. She next walked to the front door, where she intentionally took hold of the doorknob and firmly pulled it shut. She knew it was symbolic for closing the door on that chapter of her life. It was finished! With one final act, Carol and Seth traveled to see her brother and offered him their forgiveness. They knew this was Christ's will and He had graciously waited for them to come to understand that truth. It was a gift they gave not only to her brother, but also, perhaps even more largely, to themselves. Tragically, Carol's brother died from an overdose of drugs in 2014.

Carol and Seth would both tell you that everyone must find their individual way of healing—there is no cookie cutter solution. However, deliverance from the consequences of abuse is too large to be achieved by willpower alone. Carol and Seth are so thankful to have God, each other, and a rich circle of Christian friends in their journey to wholeness. Carol says, "There was a whole lot of 'tender holding' between Seth and me that was a large part of the healing. Beyond our humanness, our Chief Shepherd was embracing us in His everlasting arms." She says of her matured viewpoint of this story, "I now see the restorative process through a bigger lens, one that involves God."

Furthermore, they each confess that the largest part of their recovery came from finding their security and identity in who they are to God, instead of remaining the broken children of their past. They now thankfully sing and know at a heart level, "I am a child of God."

Seth defines a miracle as "a time when God intervenes in our lives". Their loving heavenly Father did that in a big way for these dear ones. First, by being there for them always, and then by giving them the gift of each other. Their unconditional love of each other, their willingness to fight their way through to healing, and their choice to stay close to God through the journey, altogether, brought them safely to the other side.

The first time that I met Carol and Seth, I was struck by the joy and peace in both. Shortly after that, it was my privilege to witness firsthand that they are a couple who prays--their response to any situation seems to be to turn to God. As I get to know them better, I know that my first impressions were right— Carol and Seth are anointed to love and care for people wherever they go. They were restored by unconditional love and are healing others by that same powerful means.

When asked about a verse that has encouraged both Seth and Carol, they look to the entirety of Psalm 91. When they ponder all the active verbs in this psalm, it is evident that God was faithful in executing all of them.

HE:
    PROVIDED a shelter and a refuge,

DELIVERED us from the snares,
COVERED us under his wings,
GUARDED us with his angels,
PROTECTED us because we knew His name,
ANSWERED our calls to Him,
WAS WITH us in trouble; and
RESCUED us…
ALL ALONG THE WAY!

Psalm 91 "Whoever dwells in the shelter of the Most High will rest in the shadow of the Almighty. I will say of the Lord, "He is my refuge and my fortress, my God, in whom I trust." Surely, he will save you from the fowler's snare and from the deadly pestilence. He will cover you with his feathers, and under his wings you will find refuge; his faithfulness will be your shield and rampart. You will not fear the terror of night, nor the arrow that flies by day, nor the pestilence that stalks in the darkness, nor the plague that destroys at midday. A thousand may fall at your side, ten thousand at your right hand, but it will not come near you. You will only observe with your eyes and see the punishment of the wicked. If you say, "The Lord is my refuge," and you make the Most High your dwelling, no harm will overtake you, no disaster will come near your tent. For he will command his angels concerning you to guard you in all your ways; they will lift you up in their hands, so that you will not strike your foot against a stone. You will tread on the lion and the cobra; you will trample the great lion and the serpent. "Because he loves me," says the Lord, "I will rescue him; I will protect him, for he acknowledges my name. He will call on me, and I will answer him; I will be with him in trouble, I will deliver him and honor him. With long life I will satisfy him and show him my salvation."

1 John 4:7 "Dear friends, let us love one another, for love comes from God. Everyone who loves has been born of God and knows God."

Father God, thank You that You give us Yourself and loving people to help with our journeys. Thank You for Your unconditional love which heals our wounds and for the healing and restorative tender hearts of others, especially our spouses. In Jesus name, Amen

Living in the Intersection of Heaven and Earth

Krista and Ric Zambito were approximately twenty weeks along in expecting their first child, a boy whom they planned to name Luca, short for Luciano. It was near Christmas and Krista had a routine ultrasound at the local hospital in Wheeling, West Virginia. After the test, they got a call from the hospital saying that the definition was not good on the ultrasound--they asked Ric and Krista to go to Allegheny General Hospital in Pittsburgh and have the test repeated. At that point, there was no indication that there was any kind of problem with the pregnancy.

After the ultrasound was redone, along with some other testing, this young couple was told the worst possible news. Luca had fetal hydrops, which is a life-threatening condition occurring when abnormal amounts of fluid accumulate in two or more body areas of a fetus or newborn. It is a symptom of underlying problems—in Luca's case, it was because he was not producing his own blood. Ric was shown a tube of Luca's blood, and it looked like pink Kool-Aid.

Ric and Krista began a merry-go-round of visiting different hospitals and doctors. Weekly appointments were at Allegheny General. They also had appointments in Wheeling. Over and over, they got the news that short of a miracle, Luca would not live. One doctor told them not to plan a baby shower, but rather to start planning a funeral. They were advised to terminate the pregnancy. The doctors' prediction was that if the baby did survive to birth by some slim chance, then he would be blind, deaf, and / or mentally challenged.

Both Ric and Krista were determined to keep the baby— for them, there was never a question of aborting. Ric said that one mainstay through this trying time was his mom- she encouraged them and was a bedrock of faith as they took their stand to trust God.

The family got area churches praying. Ric's uncle attended a national flooring convention and spoke to the president about Luca and the situation. This kind man made an announcement from the stage about Luca's problem and asked for the attendees to pray for him. The Zambito family began hearing of people praying all over the United States for their precious baby.

Ric remembers hearing a song on January 6th called "I Need a Miracle'. In prayer, he poured out the words from the song along with all the anguish in his heart as he screamed and cried out for help from God. A few days later, they heard about the possibility of blood transfusions for Luca.

Finally, Ric and Krista had a ray of hope. A doctor in Pittsburgh was trying transfusions for fetal hydrops. He told Ric and Krista of the dangers. If they gave too much blood during a transfusion, then Luca's heart could burst. Even though this doctor held out hope, he told them that odds that Luca would live were one in a thousand. Ric and Krista chose those odds because they trusted in their mighty God.

The Pittsburgh doctors began a series of transfusions at University of Pittsburgh McGee Women's Hospital—these took place every four weeks. They put a needle through Krista's belly and into the uterus to anesthetize Luca first, so that he would not move around during the procedure. Ultrasound was used to guide the needle for the anesthetic and the transfusion.

When they first started, Luca's hemoglobin was 1.5. It should have been at least 15. Krista and the baby were monitored at the local hospital, but also went back to Pittsburgh for careful observation and testing.

Luca received five transfusions over eighteen weeks. Accumulated fluid continued to show up indicating that the fetal hydrops was not resolved yet. Luca's hemoglobin count would improve after transfusions then drop again. Krista and Ric were on a roller coaster of emotions as they would have glimmers of hope then more heartbreak and worry. Through it all, they clung to Jesus—both found their faith growing in leaps and bounds. After the third transfusion, there were indications that Luca's hemoglobin count was starting to stabilize. Luca began to maintain the rise in hemoglobin after the treatment.

On April 20, Krista started having contractions. These became full-on labor on April 27, and Ric hurried Krista to Pittsburgh. Once there, Luca's heart rate started to drop drastically so the doctor did an emergency C-section. Luca was born at 2:06 pm on April 27, 2013.

After the birth, Krista and Ric did not get to hold or even see baby Luca—he was whisked away. His platelet count was dangerously low. His anxious parents called the prayer warriors who had been praying over this situation. They asked for very specific prayers: for Luca's hemoglobin and platelet count to become normal and to stay there. Their prayers were completely answered.

After seven days, mama and baby went home, but not long after that they began return appointments as the doctors tried to find out the root cause of Luca's problem. There was no progress on finding why fetal hydrops occurred, so Ric and Krista finally stopped the appointments. They reached their own conclusion as to why this all happened.

They had prayed for good health of mama and baby. God answered those prayers-- both Krista and Luca are healthy. Ric had also been praying for a life-changing experience. His relationship with God before all of this had been distant and impersonal—he attended church, but God was not a big part of his life.

God became very personal and important to the Zambito family. Ric prays Psalm 91 over Luca every day. Ric and Krista know for certain that God loves us. They also know that there is nothing that is impossible with God. Ric cannot overemphasize the power of prayer--he has felt and seen it firsthand.

They heard plenty of naysaying and discouraging words from the medical people, but Krista and Ric clung to their only Hope, and He delivered them. One of the doctors who had been discouraging did finally give a nod to a higher power at work when Luca became healthy.

Ric and Krista live in the intersection of heaven and earth where God's power is manifested right here and now. Heaven is present on earth for believers—it starts within us when we ask God to dwell in us as the temples of the living God. As believers, we can learn to recognize that this confluence of heaven and earth abides in us. Our eyes can be opened to God's might exhibited all around us through the power of the Holy Spirit.

Luca has his photo on billboards for the family flooring business—so I saw him there before I met him in person. The billboards with Luca always grabbed my attention, but I did not know until recently that I was looking at a miracle. Luca is eight years old now, is gorgeous, and glows with good health. Luca's parents cannot help but wonder what great purposes God has for him. He was meant to be here!

Psalm 91 "We live within the shadow of the Almighty, sheltered by the God who is above all gods. This I declare that he alone is my refuge, my place of safety; he is my God, and I am trusting him. For he rescues you from every trap and protects you from the fatal plague. He will shield you with his wings! They will shelter you. His faithful promises are your armor. Now you don't need to be afraid of the dark anymore, nor fear the dangers of the day; nor dread the plagues of darkness, nor disasters in the morning. Though a thousand fall at my side, though ten thousand are dying around me, the evil will not touch me. I will see how the wicked are punished, but I will not share it. For Jehovah is my refuge! I choose the God above all gods to shelter me. How then can evil overtake me or any plague come near? For he orders his angels to protect you wherever you go. They will steady you with their hands to keep you from stumbling against the rocks on the trail. You can safely meet a lion or step on poisonous snakes, yes, even trample them beneath your feet! For the Lord says, 'Because he loves me, I will rescue him; I will make him great because he trusts in my name. When he calls on me, I will answer; I will be with him in trouble and rescue him and honor him. I will satisfy him with a full life and give him my salvation.'"

Father, thank You for faithful parents who cling to You in the face of disaster. Thank You for healing Luca. Thank

You that you hear and respond to prayer and for Your tender and faithful love. In Jesus' name, Amen

A Modern Day Barnabas

"Many a life has come forth from the furnace of affliction more beautiful and more useful than before." Billy Graham.

In the last few years, I became friends with a modern-day hero, a Barnabas (like Paul's cohort in spreading the gospel to the Gentiles). She is a gentle but mighty soul who has been through a major furnace of affliction which has made her more beautiful and useful than before, as well as more equipped to accomplish her eternal purposes.

She is a Barnabas in the sense of being an encourager / evangelist. Barnabas means "Son of encouragement", and Betty means "Abundance of God". Both descriptions are very appropriate for my friend (except for the son part).

Betty lost her mom to liver failure. At the time no one knew what caused it, but Betty now knows it was a disease called primary biliary cholangitis or cirrhosis, which is a chronic disease that causes the bile ducts in the liver to be slowly destroyed. Bile is made by the liver, aids with digestion and helps the body get rid of cholesterol, toxins, and worn-out red blood cells.

With bile duct damage, bile backs up in the liver and can lead to irreversible scarring of liver tissue (cirrhosis). This is an autoimmune disease (meaning the immune system mistakenly attacks healthy cells in the bile ducts) but also has some genetic and environmental triggers.

This disease usually develops gradually, but in Betty's case it did not (although in her forties she had elevated liver enzymes without any other symptoms). Nonetheless,

Betty was healthy and symptom-free until she reached sixty-eight years of age when she had surgery to correct a foot problem. Prior to the surgery, her doctors found that she had bleeds in her esophagus. This was her first real indication that she was starting into liver failure. (These broken blood vessels develop when normal blood flow to the liver is blocked by clots or scar tissue. This causes increased blood flow into smaller blood vessels which can leak blood or even rupture.) Notwithstanding, it is very possible to live with liver cirrhosis for many years, so no one was greatly alarmed by this.

Slow development of liver dysfunction was not what happened with Betty—she had a trio of circumstances in 2019 that caused her liver to have more accelerated deterioration. These ended up being 'the straw that broke the camel's back' for her liver. First, she developed an abscess tooth, then a bursitis, and lastly an inflammation of her lower intestine. All of these were treated with antibiotics. Apparently, there are some antibiotics that are safer for use with damaged livers and some much less prudent ones. Betty was given a lot of the not-safe antibiotics for the treatment of these three conditions, even though her medical team were apprised of her liver issues. (This is an illustration that we all need an advocate in our current medical system.)

When Betty was in the hospital being treated for intestinal inflammation in January of 2019, her son's doctor dropped by her room. He asked if Betty was ever tested to find out the root cause of her liver problems (The answer was no.), and he suggested going to University of Pittsburgh Medical Center (UPMC). Betty was sent by ambulance to UPMC to find out more about her liver issues. The emergency vehicle driver was a Christian who gave encouragement to Betty in a similar manner to what Betty would later do for so many others. This man prayed for her and said that he felt the surety from God that Betty would be okay. This encouraging word gave Betty a measure of peace.

Going to the liver specialist in Pittsburgh was providential—UPMC found the underlying problem (Betty's genetic background and the administration of dangerous antibiotics), and she was also positioned in the best place possible for what was to come next. UPMC has done the highest number of living-donor transplant surgeries of any facility in the United States, and it is ranked by U.S. News and World Report to be the twelfth best hospital in the nation overall.

After her initial visit and hospital stay at UPMC, Betty returned two weeks later for a visit to see the doctor who was head of the department at the Center for Liver Diseases. This woman was running very late, but it turned out that Betty and her husband, Roger, had a divine appointment in the waiting room. A couple was sitting across from Betty and Roger, plus a man sat on either side of them. Because Betty is naturally friendly, she struck up conversation with those around her. The young man of the couple had a liver transplant because of a car accident—he was there for a follow up visit. The other two men were there as part of the process of becoming liver donors. Betty asked why they would do such a thing. One said, "Because God told me to do it." The other man said, "I do it for people like you." Betty and Roger were in awe of such amazing and generous people.

At that point, neither of them had any inkling that Betty would soon need a liver donated so that she could stay alive. Even though Betty was becoming critical, and the signs were right in front of them, Betty and Roger were in denial about the possibility of her needing a liver transplant. Roger later remembered the liver specialist telling Betty at this first appointment that she would probably have to get a transplant. Neither Betty nor Roger processed the information at that time.

Next began the period of rapid worsening in Betty's health. Betty grew more jaundiced (yellow from built-up bilirubin); her urine became darker and darker brown as more bile was excreted through her kidneys; and whole-body itching took over her life completely, as toxins came out through her skin (this was so intense that Betty could no longer sleep during this period). Roger, ever kind and attentive, suffered greatly with his wife and often gave her face rubs to help soothe her. He was as supportive as any spouse could possibly be—it seemed that he would gladly take on her suffering if he could have.

As Betty became more acutely ill, her appointments grew more frequent until in March, she was traveling from Wheeling to Pittsburgh twice weekly. Betty's body was in high alert trying to deal with her liver crisis. She could never relax, no matter what. All of this was burning her out quickly—she found out later that the doctors thought she could only continue in this state for three months before her body would give out completely, and she would die.

UPMC monitored Betty with extreme attention--Roger and Betty had the phone number for a coordinator whom they could call at any time. Roger tried to call the coordinator after Betty was up all night with dry heaves (Roger also remained awake, trying to soothe her by rubbing her face the whole time). In the morning, when he tried to tell the coordinator what was going on, he could not make her understand. Both Roger and Betty were so sleep deprived they could not string a coherent thought together. The coordinator told them to come to UPMC immediately, so they made another trip to Pittsburgh to get a prescription to help her dry heaves.

Periodically, because of Betty's inability to detox, ammonia would build up in her system with the primary symptom being confusion. (Another person would need to recognize this because Betty could not.) She would have to take another dreaded medicine that made her have repeated bowel movements to flush out the ammonia until it returned to safe levels.

As her liver failed more, lots of excess fluid began building up in Betty's abdomen. This had to be drained several times with a needle and syringe. Betty was extremely scared and emotional over this but got two comforting assistances from God. The first was a word from a nurse, "Do you know that getting appointments quickly like you have simply does not happen? You should thank your God." God was providing for Betty in every detail for every step of the way. The second comfort was a phrase that Betty heard over and over in her heart during the ordeal. It was God whispering to her, "I've got this Betty!" Betty could feel peace filling her as God gave his tender, nurturing love.

In the meantime, Betty's family was becoming more concerned about her decline. One of Betty's daughters-in-law, who is a dental hygienist, volunteered to be a part of the team to help with medical advice and decisions. God provided for every need, both large and small, as Betty and Roger traveled their difficult journey. They got untold support and love all along the way from family and friends which was of immeasurable value in going through their trials.

In March of 2019, Betty was at UPMC when a group of doctors came in. One of the doctors said that Betty's liver was not functioning. Roger said, "At least she does not need a liver transplant!" The doc looked at Roger and said, "Yes, she does." Roger and Betty turned to each other and started crying. Their denial was now a thing of the past, and the preparation, education, and encouragement from UPMC started in earnest. Betty was put on the nationwide registry to get a liver. These livers were either from cadavers or living donors. There were different ways to find living donors in addition to the registry, like advertising on Facebook or doing private searches among family and friends.

When Betty and Roger were alone in the room, after the bombshell was dropped about her needed transplant, Betty looked at Roger and said, "I bet it will be Gina." That was a prophetic word. Jay, Betty's son, and Gina, Jay's wife, had been praying about being a donor for Betty. Both were O positive, like Betty, which met the first criteria. They also met the age requirement of being younger than fifty-five. They were thirty-seven years old and in great physical shape. Much more testing was required before either could qualify to donate part of their liver. Meetings with a social worker and a counselor, having heart and body system checks, and age and weight requirements were just a part of the procedures. Rigorous testing on many fronts must be passed before there was a green light. Gina was the first one to go through the battery of tests—she did them all in one day. If she did not meet the requirements, then Jay would be tested.

Gina was deemed a good match. Betty would never have asked anyone to give part of their liver—the surgery and recovery are a big deal. Although the person's liver usually regrows to its normal size after a few months, the recovery process can be slow and tough. (Amazingly, the portions of liver grow to the size the organ was in each individual person before the transplant)

Betty did her best to make sure that Gina was sure about being a living donor. Betty even called Gina's parents and talked to them. "This is what it means to lay down your life for another, but this is your baby girl," Betty said to them. Gina's mom and dad told Betty that Gina felt like God wanted her to do this. Nothing could deter her— she was one hundred and fifty per cent sure. Gina's parents were also behind her one hundred and fifty percent. This God-loving woman told her family that she would always choose obedience to God over expediency—this was a lesson deeply ingrained in her heart.

When Easter rolled around, the extended family got together. One of the grandkids looked at Betty's eyes and commented to another family member, "Grandma's eyes are so yellow, they look like they were colored with a marker."

Meanwhile, Gina was communicating with UPMC. They told her that the surgery needed to happen quickly because Betty was declining fast. Shortly after that, Betty got a call from Gina, "Pack your bags, I am giving you a liver on May 1!" After all the pain and suffering that seemed like it would never end, Roger and Betty cried with relief for three solid hours after hearing Gina's news.

Betty was instructed to isolate so that she would stay healthy, but three days before she was to go to UPMC, her ammonia levels rose dangerously. Betty got into the car, vomited, and then could not remember anything after that. Poor Roger kept rubbing her face as he drove—he was afraid that he was losing her. When they got to UPMC, it took five doses of the medicine to bring Betty out of this crisis. It was a miserable time, and Roger told the doctors that he was not taking Betty home. It was too scary for Roger and Betty to deal with each of these crises. Betty stayed at UPMC until her surgery and was moved to the surgery floor the night before it would take place. It was now at the end of April.

Roger would not leave Betty—he slept in an uncomfortable chair to be right there for her. The night before the surgery, Roger asked Betty what she wanted to do. She said the only thing she wanted was a dance with him. They danced in her hospital room to Elvis Presley, as the nurses kept dropping by to see this wondrous testament of love. On this same night before the surgery, Betty was given a vision from God of big angel wings over both surgical rooms. Nothing negative or hurtful would get past those wings.

Betty was up early in the morning and walking the hall. She saw another family in the hallway and heard them talking about also getting a transplant that day. Betty began praying under her breath for them, and the man of the family heard her and stopped to talk to her. Betty told him that she prayed for them and had the sense that it would turn out well. He became teary and thanked her.

Gina was to have her surgery start first, so that the timing would be right to get the donated liver portion quickly into Betty. Before Gina drove to the hospital, her sweet and faith-filled son left a bunch of encouraging Bible verses taped around the bathroom so she would read them right before she left for the hospital. Right before Gina's surgery began, Betty did get wheeled into the pre-op area to say hi to Gina.

On the way to her surgical room, Betty made a comment about God, and the young man who was with her asked if she would like someone to pray with her. Betty replied in the affirmative, so he showed her a list of some names from which she could choose. Betty chose the head of anesthesiology to come and pray with her. After he showed up and prayed, he asked why she had chosen him. She told him, "You had a lot of letters after your name, but you have humbled yourself before God." This doctor told Betty what an honor it was to pray for her.

Both surgeries went according to plan. Betty's surgery lasted longer than Gina's (seven hours) and when they took her old liver out, it was green. Recovery room time was five to six hours long—when Betty finally came to, she had on an oxygen mask. They let her take it off and have some ice chips, both of which were unspeakably wonderful for Betty.

Later, when Betty was back in her room on the surgical ward, the doctor popped in to say that she was 'queen of the floor' because she was doing so well. In Betty's next step towards going home, the physical therapist dropped by to have Betty walk and go up and down steps. Apparently, Betty was not quite ready for this and started bleeding (bloody diarrhea). They had to take her back to surgery to stop the bleeding. Because of the extra repair surgery Betty's total time in the hospital was ten days— Gina's hospital stay was four days.

The recovery was slow and painful—it was during her prolonged healing phase that I first met Betty. When she came home from the hospital, Betty was on twenty-seven pills. Her docs have since gradually decreased her meds as they safely could, and Betty is back to her full life and exercise. Betty now lifts weights and walks miles—she has always been very physically active. Her blood test results have been somewhat up and down since her surgery, but they now seem to have stabilized and are very good.

I saved the best of the story until last. You could see snippets of Betty's prayer and encouragement for people all through the story, but there was so much more. Betty told tale after tale of ministering to people all through the period of her own suffering and surgeries. Here are just a few.

As she was waiting to get the fluid drained from her abdomen a second time, Betty heard a young man two beds away sighing repeatedly. She prayed for him and sang to him, then said, "I want you to know about God's love—he has you in the palm of his hand." The young man thanked her. She felt the Holy Spirit urge her to go on, "I don't know where you have been and what you have done. I don't care and neither does God." The young man started weeping uncontrollably, and Betty knew that the Holy Spirit was ministering to his heart.

Another time, an orderly was wheeling Betty to a test. She began asking her usual questions, "Where do you live? What do you do?" He told her he was a video game developer in a very competitive field, and he did the orderly job to put food on the table. Betty asked, "Can I pray for you?" After she did, God gave her encouragement to speak to him, "God is going to bless your life in a mighty way. You will rise up in this industry." Betty spoke life and light into him which he sorely needed. He began weeping and saying repeatedly, "I will never forget you!"

While Betty was in a hospital room, a woman came regularly to clean her space. One day Betty had on worship music. (She often did this, and it ministered to many.). The woman began singing along with the song, which led to a conversation. The woman seemed somewhat mentally impaired, and she told Betty what a hard time she was having getting her driver's license because of being a slow learner. Betty told this woman how important she was. The hospital and patients needed her and depended on her. She was crucial and valued. This seemed to be just what she needed to hear from the Holy Spirit through Betty's words, and she continued with her work with a more courageous attitude.

Betty learned lots through this time of suffering. She became more loving towards God and people, more empathetic, and she realized more how much little things mean. (A card, a kind word, an encouraging Facebook post.) She used to be too busy to take time in these little details, but purification in the furnace of fiery trials gave Betty a willingness to see and hear people. She now takes the time. She prays the prayers. She speaks encouragement. She has a very thankful heart and spreads that gratitude everywhere she goes.

Betty says, "As God reveals himself to you, that is what we have to give to others." That is how Betty now lives her life. She listens, watches, and when she sees any move on God's part, she quickly moves in obedience. This brings a living, breathing (but female) Barnabas to life in a constant ministry wherever the Holy Spirit leads the way.

Please note that I did not use real names in this story. Here is the reason for that: although this story is completely true, none of the principal people, including Betty and Gina, want to take any glory or credit from God. Regarding this, Betty stated, "When God gives you a gift, the enemy will tell you all kind of lies about that gift. He tells me that I am bragging when I speak about it, and I should keep silent. That is where my spiritual battle is right now. Yet, these stories about our good and loving Father need to be out there."

Acts 11:22-24. "The news about them reached the ears of the church at Jerusalem, and they sent Barnabas off to Antioch. Then when he arrived and witnessed the grace of God, he rejoiced and began to encourage them all with resolute heart to remain true to the Lord; for he was a good man, and full of the Holy Spirit and of faith. And considerable numbers were brought to the Lord."

Father, thank You for the encouragers who bring Your light and life everywhere they go. I am so sad that Betty and Roger had to suffer so much to become such powerful tools in your hand, but I am also very grateful for the people that they have become. In Jesus' name, Amen

Valley of the Shadow of Death

Steve and Linda Smith are in their seventies, but you would never know it. They look remarkably young, but their activities belie their ages even more than their appearance. Steve does numerous hands-on mission trips with a disaster recovery organization called Eight Days of Hope. He has also been involved in a spin-off ministry to build or remodel half-way houses for victims of sex trafficking. Steve has been on at least thirty-six missions, and Linda has gone on some as well.

Steve has a reputation at our church of being a 'go-to guy'. He is the crazy guy who never stops and who can do anything. When I say he does hands-on ministry, that means he goes into places where there have been floods, tornadoes, or any sort of disaster, and he helps to rebuild things. He charges into the worst possible places and situations and makes them better.

Up until June of 2019, Steve's energy and reserves seemed limitless. Then, at seventy-two years old, he went to see his family doctor in Wheeling, West Virginia. He told her, "I don't feel right--always exhausted and having to take naps. I have never done that. Also, I have a hacking cough that won't go away." The doctor told him that it was probably viral and would be cleared up before the tests came back. She ordered a chest x-ray and bloodwork.

When those test results came back, there was concern about something on the x-ray, so the doctor ordered a CT scan and sent Steve to a pulmonologist at Wheeling Hospital. While undergoing the tests, Steve did not improve—he became even weaker and more exhausted. The CT scan showed the same thing that was on the x-rays—there was a mass in the lungs. The pulmonologist also looked at the films from a PET scan that had just been done on Steve—the radiologist's report was not done yet. She told Linda and Steve that cancer cells light up In a PET scan—Steve not only had the area in his lung that was bright on the PET scan but also areas around the kidneys, trunk, and abdomen. This doctor was going on vacation but wanted to do a bronchoscopy to get a biopsy of the lung mass when she came back. She told Linda and Steve that they could tell from the biopsy what stage it was.

What Linda heard loud and clear from what the doctor said (and did not say) during the visit was CANCER, and Linda was terrified. This was her precious husband who had been her other half for more than forty years. He was so much a part of who she was that she could not even remember laughing out loud before he came into her life.

The idea of Steve being very ill was a much scarier possibility than if she faced major illness herself.

Within the family, there were some medical resources. Steve's niece is a nationally recognized pediatrician, and her husband, John, is an infectious disease doctor. John agreed that the mass could be cancer but told them that the location in Steve's lung would make it difficult to do a biopsy. He also brought up the possibility of the mass being a fungal infection from Steve's disaster relief work around stagnant water and filth.

Steve's health steadily worsened with his naps increasing to four a day. His doctor had determined that he did have some type of viral infection that was contributing to his fatigue, but the possible cancer in Steve's lung had Linda sobbing secretly in the basement by the dryer where Steve would not hear her.

It felt to Linda like they needed a second opinion, so she prayed for God to open doors so Steve could be seen, receive an accurate diagnosis, and be given effective treatment. Steve was too weak to take charge--he had no fight left in him. However, Linda had enough for both of them, so during one of Steve's naps she called Cleveland Clinic. Linda connected to a woman named Val who was to schedule an appointment with the pulmonology department. Val told Linda that she could get Steve in for a second opinion in August—that was two whole months away with a possible cancer diagnosis!

When Linda heard how far out the earliest available appointment was, she burst into tears and said, "I don't know what to do. A two month wait with a possible cancer diagnosis is terrifying." Val began working to find an earlier appointment--numerous times Val asked Linda to hold the line while she worked on getting Steve in earlier. Miraculously, an appointment time opened for him just four days later, on June 17th. An answered prayer for sure, it felt like the right course.

When Steve got up from his nap, Linda said, "We are going to Cleveland Clinic, number two in the nation. If you aren't happy with that, I will call Mayo Clinic and get you into number one."

The night before Steve and Linda drove to Cleveland for the appointment, twelve elders from the church came to their house to pray for Steve. They anointed him with oil and prayed for his healing just as the Bible instructs. This time of prayer gave Linda a tremendous peace. (Steve had been unflappable the whole time. His attitude was, "If I die, I go to a better place, and when it is my time to die then it will happen." He did not want to leave Linda or his loved ones, but none of this health crisis disrupted his peace or joy.)

Linda and Steve drove to Cleveland and stayed with one of their sons who lives there. Their son drove them the next day to the appointment. When they saw the doctor, their son made the comment that the doc shuffled when he walked. He was older and very experienced. The doctor looked at the CT scan, the bloodwork, took a medical history, and did an exam. He told Linda and Steve that their department did not use PET scans for diagnostic work—there were too many factors that could give false information. He also asked Steve to tell him more about his acid reflux and hiatal hernia--Steve replied that he had it for years and had an elevated bed to help keep his stomach contents from coming back up into his throat.

The doctor left the room a few times to consult with a radiologist then at the end of his examination, he said, "I don't think you have cancer. Possibly from aspirating food from your acid reflux, we think you have an infection and pneumonia. With treatment from antibiotics, you should feel like a new person in a few days."

Steve is a naturally optimistic person, so he had not taken the possible cancer diagnosis to heart. Linda is a prepare for the future type lady, and she had been fearful that her beloved one was facing some type of lung cancer. When they left the appointment at Cleveland Clinic, Linda felt like they were both given new life.

At the return appointment, Steve did not even greet the doctor before joyfully blurting out, "You were right!" The antibiotic had made him feel like a new man. Within days of being on the medication, Steve was putting in a retaining wall, digging, and lifting seventy-pound blocks. He also was back to his no-naps self. The repeat CT scan showed just a slight cloudiness where the mass had been.

Steve has returned to his 'nothing can stop me' way of life. I fully expect to see him doing missions as well as any work that God assigns him for decades to come.

Psalm 23: 4 "Yea, though I walk through the valley of the shadow of death, I will fear no evil: for thou art with me; thy rod and thy staff they comfort me."

Father, thank You for staying with us when we are shadowed by disease and death. Thank You for being our good shepherd. Also, we are so grateful for the medical people that You use to help us, especially when they are experienced and wise. You can heal us with a word, or You can use any means. You are in control, and we trust You. In Jesus' name, Amen

Never Be Afraid to Ask

Sarah Smith is a new acquaintance, but when we first spoke, I immediately knew that I was in the presence of someone who is very wise before her time—an old soul in a young body. Sarah has a blog entitled 'This Glorious Wait', which I perused before having our interview for this story. (You can read her blog at thisgloriouswait.wordpress.com. It is my plan to read it again and again for its valid and very applicable truth.) It is occasionally heart-wrenching, but a worthwhile investment of time. In the blog we learn about the Smith household. They are living examples of how to handle the harshest of circumstances with grace, and how to find meaning and joy in the most ordinary events.

Five-and-one-half years ago, Sarah and Preston welcomed their second child, a baby girl named Evelyn, into their family. She only lived for twenty days after her birth. They never got a clear diagnosis— only a vague reference to anoxia that caused brain damage without an understanding of the root cause.

Here is a quote from Sarah's blog. "When Evelyn was alive, we prayed. Oh, how we prayed. It felt as if we prayed without ceasing, pleading with God to heal her because we know that he is able. And you know what? He did. He is faithful and full of mercy. The moment she set foot on eternity's shore, she was whole and perfectly healed. Her first steps took her straight into the arms of Jesus. She bypassed the difficulties and pain of this world, and she entered her forever, heavenly home. I'm not sad for her. I'm just really sad for us because we're left behind, waiting, until Jesus calls us home someday too."

Many others also prayed for Evelyn and the whole Smith family. Sarah speaks about the effects of these prayers, "We were strengthened. We were filled with hope. We were surrounded with peace. We were able to make painfully courageous decisions, only because the Lord Himself was walking with us, showing us the way to go as we approached each new fork in the road."

She elaborated, "If we didn't know Jesus, we would not have made it through. We might have become bitter. Our marriage might have fallen apart. God gave us hope."

Of course, the grieving process is a lifelong journey. It cannot be short-circuited even when you know your baby is with Jesus. Sarah told me that when she started writing her blog, she needed people to see that Evelyn's life mattered. Blogging helped her process her grief, but then the writing gradually morphed into something more—a place to share what God was revealing. (In between Evelyn's death and the event that is the subject of this tale, Sarah and Preston went through other amazing events like adopting their third child, a newborn son, and they gave birth to another son. Talk about miracles. However, we will stick to the story at hand.)

Scarlett Smith was born on October 14, 2020, as the Smith's fifth child. The Smiths now have three sons, one daughter on earth, and one daughter in heaven. All seemed fine with Scarlett until Sarah started noticing some odd movements and facial expressions when Scarlett was about five months old. (You can search for Infantile Spasms on YouTube to see what they look like. Some of her symptoms involved contractions of her tummy, arms, and legs, a wincing face, a change in demeanor, and a sudden head drop, along with fussing.) Sarah took Scarlett to the pediatrician, who thankfully knew that there was reason for concern. He told Sarah about his suspicion of Infantile Spasms (IS). (The symptoms that Scarlett was having are often written off as colic, startle reflexes, or just normal baby actions.) Once Sarah and Preston knew there was a real problem, they talked to two family members over the weekend, both of whom work in the medical field. One of them is a nurse in the Emergency Department at Children's Hospital in Pittsburgh. She showed the video of Scarlett's spasms to her ED colleagues and then advised Sarah and Preston to bring her to the Emergency Department right away.

During the drive to Children's Hospital of UPMC, neither Sarah nor Preston said a word to each other. Yes, they were scared, but more than that, they were looking to see the continuation of God's work in their lives. In Sarah's mind, she was picturing angels leading the charge, going before them, and surrounding them, while the song 'The Battle Belongs to You' by Phil Wickham was playing in her head. The beginning lyrics proclaim, "When all I see is the battle, You see my victory. When all I see is the mountain, You see a mountain moved. And as I walk through the shadow, Your love surrounds me. There's nothing to fear now for I am safe with You." There was no doubt that the Lord was with them. His peace and presence were very evident.

Once they had Scarlett at the Emergency Department, things happened quickly. Sarah recounted the events, "Within forty-eight hours Scarlett was admitted, diagnosed and started a treatment called ACTH (adrenocorticotropic hormone). Her spasms stopped by day three of the medication. During this four-week series of injections, her brain basically rebooted and resolved the spasms. Scarlett does not have to return for more treatment at all, only a three-month follow-up with the neurologist. Although there is a small chance of relapse or the possibility of another epileptic disorder developing down the road, the Smiths feel hopeful that Scarlett will continue to thrive. It's common for babies with IS to experience a variety of developmental delays, but with the help of a local early intervention program, Scarlett will receive the help she needs to catch up on some of her motor development. As one of her doctors put it, "Let's hope all of this is just a little hiccup in her journey.""

The story that I just told you was miracle enough and we could stop right there. However, this amazing family does not just look at surface things. Sarah is a student of the Bible and strives to see with spiritual eyes and hear with spiritual ears. She delved into two consecutive passages of scripture from Mark 10:35-52 where two groups of people asked Jesus for very specific things. Jesus asked each of them the same question, "What do you want me to do for you?" Then He answered them both in surprising ways.

In the first passage, his disciples, James, and John, had a bold request for Jesus. Jesus asked them, "What do you want me to do for you?" The two disciples told him that they wanted honor and glory in Jesus's kingdom of heaven, "Let one of us sit at your right and the other at your left in your glory" (Mark 10:37). In response, Jesus told them that if they wanted to be great In His Kingdom, they must become servants. If they wanted glory, they needed to lay down their lives in service of others. The answer was quite unexpected. Yes, they could be great, but the path to greatness in Christ's kingdom wasn't exactly what the disciples were envisioning. Being great meant serving. Being first meant being last. It all felt a little upside down, but ultimately Jesus would make them great if they lived lives of humble service to Him.

In the very next passage, it tells of a blind man named Bartimaeus who persistently called out to Jesus. "What do you want me to do for you?" asked Jesus. The blind man answered him, "Rabbi, I want to see." Immediately Jesus healed him. The blind man made a specific request and Jesus answered exactly the way he had expected. Simple as that.

Sarah felt like God brought this passage to her mind to help her faith grow as she sorted through the questions and complexities of her two daughters' stories. Both of their baby girls were diagnosed with brain issues but experienced very different journeys and outcomes.

Evelyn's diagnosis was vague with no known cause, while Scarlett's diagnosis was clearly determined right away. Evelyn's body struggled to perform basic life functions and her condition slowly declined since no medication could make her better, while Scarlett showed improvement almost immediately once she started her treatment. Evelyn died, and Scarlett lived.

With both of their daughters, the Smiths asked God to heal them. And yet each girl experienced a different outcome. Or so it seems.

In the same way that Jesus gave James and John an unexpected, somewhat complicated "yes" answer, He also gave a similar "yes" answer to Evelyn. He did heal her, totally and completely. It just wasn't a healing that took place on earth, like the Smiths had desired. Her perfect healing occurred in heaven, where she is now truly whole and well. Instead of an immediate "yes", Evelyn received her ultimate "yes".

And just like Jesus gave Bartimaeus a simple "yes", so too He gave Scarlett a simple, immediate healing. He was blind, then he could see. Scarlett was having seizures and now she's not.

Although Evelyn and Scarlett had different stories with different outcomes, in both cases there was still a happy ending. However, sometimes the happy ending is visible to us in the here and now. Other times, the happy ending takes place in heaven.

No matter what difficulty you're facing, never be afraid to ask God for what you want. He is a perfect heavenly father who loves you so much. He will not give a stone or snake when you ask for bread or fish (Luke 11:9-13). His answers always come from a heart of love, even when they aren't exactly what we thought they would be. Ultimately, He gives Himself to us so that we are never alone in our trials, and we can be filled with hope because He promises that one day there will surely be a happy ending.

What is a miracle to Sarah personally? "It is a display of God's power. To me this means that Jesus always gives us a happy ending, whether it's immediate or ultimate. Whatever we suffer in this lifetime cannot compare to the weight of glory we will have in heaven (2 Corinthians 4:17)."

Psalm 18:6 "In my distress I called to the Lord; I cried to my God for help. From his temple he heard my voice; my cry came before him, into his ears."

Father God, You always hear us, and You always answer. Just like You gave Sarah and Preston eyes to see Your answer that was not visible to their physical eyes, give us those spiritual eyes so we can trust that You answer us in the best possible way. You love us and You answer us with an eventual happy ending, always! In Jesus' name, Amen

Living on Bonus Time

Darryl and Judy Crews are in the same church small group as Lee and me. Darryl is an excellent teacher, both as his profession, and as a Bible scholar. Darryl also happens to be one of the humblest men that I know. A few years back, he had major health issues, and our whole small group was praying big-time.

In November of 2019, Darryl was on an entrance ramp to get on Interstate 70 with a car in front of him. All the sudden, something weird happened to Darryl. He saw that he was going to hit the car ahead of him, but he could not stop it from happening. That was the instant that Darryl lost consciousness. His car was extensively damaged and needed to be towed. The other driver was able to drive away with minimal damage. Both seemed to be unhurt.

However, Darryl quickly started having visual changes. His ophthalmologist saw him immediately to examine his eyes and contacted his GP, who then hospitalized Darryl for tests. They found the following problems with testing: a pulmonary embolism, a blood clot in Darryl's knee, twenty to thirty percent blockage of the carotid artery, and seventy to eighty percent blockage of the intracranial artery in his brain. The only option for the major brain vessel obstruction looked to be surgery at some point. It also seemed scary that so many blockages were happening. Why was all of this occurring and what could be done?

Before moving ahead, Darryl and Judy did two things. First, they called the elders of our church together to pray for healing. Second, they scheduled to go to Cleveland Clinic to get a second opinion. At Cleveland Clinic, the tests were repeated. This time the tests miraculously showed only twenty to thirty percent blockage in the brain blood vessel. Darryl was told that no intervention was needed--he could go home.

Did the medical people agree that a miracle took place as Darryl and Judy explained it to them? Judging from their responses, probably not. However, Darryl and Judy knew that it was God's hand. All of us who prayed diligently for him and who saw the sharp turnaround in his health also knew that a miracle took place. Once Darryl had the elders pray for him out of obedience to the Bible's instructions, things seemed to drastically improve. Is it possible that just such a step of obedience brought about big healing in Darryl's body?

Darryl continued his story with the shocking statement, "I am living on bonus time anyway."

He told me of getting a kidney stone in his right kidney eleven years ago. When they tested and found the kidney stone, they also found kidney cancer.

The doctor told Darryl how 'lucky' he was. By the time kidney cancer begins to show symptoms, it is invariably too late to treat it. (Darryl observed this to be true, as one of his buddies did start having kidney cancer symptoms and was diagnosed with kidney carcinoma. He was dead within a year.)

After Darryl's kidney cancer was diagnosed, his GP made arrangements for him to go to Cleveland Clinic. The typical treatment for kidney cancer is to remove the whole kidney. By God's grace, the Crews found a doctor in Cleveland who did it differently. He removed the outer third of Darryl's kidney. The doc told Darryl that he would never have problems with it again. Darryl has not had any recurrence or issues with his kidney, just as the doctor predicted.

Another huge outcome from this is that Darryl and Judy often share about his 'bonus time'. It opens opportunities to talk about the goodness of God.

James 5:14. Is anyone among you sick? Let them call the elders of the church to pray over them and anoint them with oil in the name of the Lord.

Thank You, Father, for preserving Darryl's life. He has taught, mentored, and expanded Your kingdom while living on bonus time. Thank You for his obedience in asking the elders to pray. Thank You for Your healing touch. In Jesus' name, Amen

Not a Tame God

If there is one truth that I have learned about God through the years of being his child, it is what C. S. Lewis says in the Chronicles of Narnia, "who said anything about safe? 'Course he isn't safe. But he's good. He's the King, I tell you.[23]" We cannot put God in a box—he is powerful and will not be contained or limited in any way. He is in no way 'a tame God'. Our very real and fervent prayers plus God's power can be an explosive combination, and the results may be more far reaching than we could ever imagine.

This story was told to me by Ivy Nsofor who has been a long-time mentor and friend to me. Ivy came with her family from Nigeria while her husband got his PHD at Trinity Divinity School. When I met and became friends with Ivy, my crash course on prayer ensued. Ivy's life was one big prayer—being friends with her was like being an intern learning how to weave prayer into every aspect of my life. Her husband, Fyne, was also mighty in the art of communicating with God.

The events in this tale took place in January of 1999 when Ivy, Fyne, and their four children still lived in Nigeria. Ivy's mother had been ill since August, but around January 24, she became acutely ill with severe complications of hypertension and high blood sugar. Ivy traveled to take her mother to the hospital in Owerri for what she thought was a heart problem, but the doctors found that it was nerve related. Her mother was admitted to the hospital, and Ivy, her brother, and his ex-fiancée stayed also. They slept in her room to make sure all her needs were met. Ivy was the constant guardian of her mom, leaving only to get meals. Every evening Ivy's husband, Fyne, came by to pray for her mom and the others in the hospital.

Because Ivy's mom was extremely ill, her hospital stay was extended. With Ivy being there around the clock, she became good friends with the nurses. If something was going on, the nurses shared it with Ivy, who did not hesitate to ask them questions about anything she wanted to know.

One day she heard loud crying and yelling on the next higher floor. She found out from the nurses the next day that a woman with sickle cell anemia had died during the night. The loud crying was this woman's mother mourning and praying as her daughter slipped into a coma prior to her death. Ivy discovered from the nurses that the woman who passed away was a woman she knew from a church they had attended previously. It saddened her that she had not gone upstairs to pray for her--the fragility of life was so much more obvious in that place.

Two days later the nurses were bustling about, and Ivy asked them what was happening. They explained that a mother had given birth to a stillborn child. The mom was still getting care, and the baby was wrapped up (for the father to pick the body up for burial).

Meanwhile, Ivy's mom was not getting better, so Ivy and Fyne prayed especially fervent pleas to God when Fyne came that evening. To Ivy's heart, their intercessions for her mom and the others in the hospital seemed very effective. Ivy looked for her mom to start improving because she felt in her spirit that the prayer had brought about some sort of change. Later Ivy sensed another stir in the hospital indicating that something was happening, so she stopped a nurse to inquire about it. The nurse told her that the baby wrapped for burial had started to move. They unwrapped it to find the dead child now alive. Ivy asked when it happened—it turned out that the baby came to life right during the time that Fyne and Ivy prayed together. Fyne and Ivy's fervent prayers for her mom and others in the hospital brought the baby to life through the Holy Spirit's response to their pleas for healing, even though they did not specifically ask for the baby to be revived. However, it was apparently time for Ivy's mother to go home to the Lord--the next day on February 4, 1999, Ivy's mom died.

James 5:16 "The prayer of a righteous person is powerful and effective."

Father, thank You that You give us the answers that are needed and not necessarily what we ask for when we pray. You know best and You can use our prayers for mighty purposes. In Jesus' name, Amen

Step by Step

One of our pastors had an atypical miracle in his life—a progression of healing which took place over a year. In the fall of 1999, Tim Orr woke up in his Florida home not feeling well. There was a scheduled breakfast with some friends and Tim went, thinking he would start feeling better. Afterwards they went to a boat show, and Tim progressed to feel even worse. He had burning and tingling in his arms and legs, plus strangely it felt like he had hot blood coursing through his body.

That night he tried to relax and sleep but finally at 1:00 am he went to the emergency department. The doctor examined him and said Tim needed to see a neurologist.

When Tim saw the neurologist, the doctor did every test imaginable—all kinds of bloodwork, MRIs of Tim's spine and brain. He was very thorough in his testing, then he sent Tim on to a rheumatologist to see if there were autoimmune issues.

Tim felt so bad that he was sure he was dying, but every test came back okay. After the brain MRI, Tim was so relieved that as he checked out at a store, he told the cashier who asked how he was doing, "It's a great day—I don't have a brain tumor!"

Even though he was happy to get good test results, Tim still felt completely terrible. It felt like he had the flu all the time, and the sensation of having hot blood persisted.

He continued to see western doctors and tried everything. His neurologist said that the problem was stress and suggested relaxation therapy, which Tim did with no real change. He was tested for food sensitivities, and they found twelve that were culprits. Tim took them all out of his diet—it seemed mildly helpful. His chiropractor found some misalignments and did adjustments. Tim ate cleanly and got back to his college weight—he started working out and got into great shape. Yet, he still felt bad.

He tried chelation therapy to remove toxins and had his mercury fillings removed. He had some periods of feeling better; his skin improved; and some long-standing gastrointestinal issues got better. Still, nothing helped the hot blood sensation or the flu-like symptoms. The bad feelings always came back.

One good thing is that Tim was able to continue working at his job during this whole period. (This preceded the turning point when Tim changed careers to become a pastor.) Tim loathed weekends as he felt every awful sensation without work to distract him. About five months into this time of sickness, Tim tried to go to a movie with a friend—he had to leave because sitting in the movie was such misery.

Tim heard about some women at church who had gone to an acupuncturist. Tim was willing to try anything, so he got the address and made an appointment. This man turned out to be a nice, humble man who spoke mostly Mandarin with a little broken English. He began the first session by asking Tim to look at his tongue. When he saw Tim's tongue, his eyes got wide and he said, "You have hot lung (Tim had asthma as a child) and hot blood. Take time but we can help."

Tim was amazed that someone finally understood his hot blood feeling. Each time the Chinese man did a treatment, he found trigger points and put the needles there. It would hurt at first then release. He hooked up electricity to go through the needles, and for about 30 minutes Tim would feel good, then the symptoms would return. These treatments continued one time a week for a series of eight treatments. Because of a big storm, Tim had to cancel an appointment. When it was time to reschedule a week later, he realized that he no longer had the awful sensations.

Tim summarizes this period in this way, "I was a believer, and this time drew me closer to the Lord and greatly increased my dependence on Him. I prayed a lot. At times, the only thing I felt I could do was pray. At that time, I did (and still do) believe in miracles. I asked the Lord to heal me repeatedly, and there were also a few times that I asked Him to take me home to be with him if I continued to feel so sick. Things got 'real' in a hurry, and it deepened my relationship with the Lord tremendously." Tim had a brief recurrence of the hot blood after he was in a taxi that was rear-ended about a year later. Apparently, the whiplash from the accident activated the same misalignment in his neck and caused the hot blood feeling again. Tim has since learned to manage his neck and had no more issues.

Is this a real miracle? You be the judge. If you have never been inflicted with pain that goes on and on without end in sight; if you have not visited so many medical people that you have lost count; if you have not had many people look askance at you like you are crazy with your weird illness that does not resolve; then you might not understand why it feels like a miracle. God did not give instantaneous resolution, "You are healed!" Nonetheless, did he not guide Tim step by step back to wellness?

We have a tenderhearted God who works by many means. Step by step Tim got well and that is no small thing—it is a miracle.

Philippians 4:19 "And my God will meet all your needs according to the riches of his glory in Christ Jesus."

Father, You can heal us with a word, yet sometimes we struggle so much to stay in good health. You can use those times to remind us how we depend upon You. You can also use a humble, Mandarin-speaking acupuncturist. Thank You for these times which deepen our faith and mature us in ways that only suffering can do. In Jesus' name, Amen

Lee's Miracle (McLaughlin family story)

This story is about my sweet husband, Lee, as an eleven year-old boy. We did not know each other then, but I am sure I can describe him accurately.

Lee was a tall, sturdy boy—active, extremely kind, and curious (with a touch of mischief). No doubt, his teachers loved him, even as they were stretched to the limit to keep ahead of him. Any teacher with wisdom knew to give Lee a challenge or a goal to reach, otherwise he got bored, because regular schoolwork was easy for him. He never tried to cause trouble, but if he was not getting a good workout of his mind then Lee became a bit of a class clown.

In November of Lee's sixth grade year, he got very sick. It started after he had a bowl of tomato soup at school. (Just the thought of tomato soup made him nauseous for years after that.) Lee had to rush to the bathroom to vomit and was then sent home. The teacher and Lee's parents thought he had a virus, however, day after day Lee kept getting more ill with lots of abdominal pain, nausea, and a low fever. (This all happened in November of 1963. During Lee's sick-time at home, President Kennedy was shot and killed—this forever put a timestamp on his illness.)

The McLaughlin's had a wonderful family doctor, Dr. Niehaus, who made house calls. He repeatedly came to their home to see Lee. The doc did all the tests, but it did not look like appendicitis. Finally, when Lee could no longer straighten up or walk well because of pain, Dr. Niehaus said, "I am admitting him to the hospital and doing surgery. We will start out by looking at his appendix."

Lee would not let them carry him to the car, despite his bent-over, stumbling gait—the poor kid was in total agony. Here is a sad detail that gives you a clue to Lee's character. Lee's parents were rushing to get Lee into the car and to the hospital, and Lee's mom accidentally slammed the door on Lee's fingers. This mishap totally broke Lee's mom because she was already stressed out beyond her limit. Alice burst into tears because she had added misery to her poor son's body. Lee started comforting her from the back seat. "It's okay Mom. Don't cry. I'll be all right."

Immediately, upon his arrival at the hospital, Lee was rushed into surgery with Dr. Niehaus. Dr. N made the incision where Lee's appendix should have been. Lee's appendix was tucked underneath his intestines, which is why there was not local tenderness or guarding when the doctor tested previously.

To get to Lee's appendix, the doctor had to enlarge the incision. When he tried to get the appendix out from under the intestines, it burst. Dr. Niehaus diligently cleaned it up, as best he could. Lee had a large incision with a deep drain in his right abdomen. This excellent doctor was heartbroken that this happened on his watch, and he apologized to Lee's parents for missing the diagnosis. He also told them that he was not sure Lee would pull through. As a parent, I can only imagine the complete anguish of Lee's mom and dad at this news (plus seeing the physical torment of their son as he fought off massive infection at this critical juncture).

Lee's mom stayed in the hospital with him, even during the nighttime. She slept in a chair to be nearby.

The second night was the most critical stage, the crucial apex of Lee's recovery. The doctor told Lee's parents that this was his make-it-or-break-it time. If he survived this night, his chances were looking up. Lee's mother was alone with her son at this pivotal point, and of course, she was in major distress. She was praying fervently and constantly until she finally fell into an exhausted sleep. Later, during this night, Lee's mother awakened and saw someone doing a doctor's exam of Lee using a stethoscope. When she was awake and alert, she realized that it was her father, Lee's grandad, who was doing the examination. Alice's father, Dr. Levi Kahle, had been a physician. He had been dead for 10 years!

Alice said, "Dad, what are you doing here?"

Her father replied, "It's all right Alice. Go back to sleep. He will be fine."

And he was fine. When Lee awoke the next morning, his fever had broken, and he was acting more like a normal boy. Alice told him about the nighttime visit of his granddad. As kids often do, Lee took that right in stride.

They withdrew the drain in Lee's right abdomen a little each day, pulling it to a shallower position. Lee missed a total of six weeks of school and had a heck of a tough recovery. Amazingly, other than avoiding rough play for another two weeks after his return to school, Lee quickly went back to a normal kid's life.

And here is the icing on the cake. God is the God of details. Later, as a college student, Lee worked at Peterson Nursing Home as an orderly. Dr. Niehaus came to see patients there weekly. When he showed up, he would send a nurse to get Lee. Effectively, he would do rounds with Lee as his apprentice (even though Lee was not a medical student). Lee loved it, and I think he had a bit of hero worship for this kind and caring doctor.

Isaiah 41:10. "So do not fear, for I am with you; do not be dismayed, for I am your God. I will strengthen you and help you; I will uphold you with my righteous right hand."

Thanks, Lord, for the miracle of saving my amazing Lee. Thank You for your comfort to his mom, Alice. Thank You for her diligent prayers and faith. In Jesus' name, Amen

Patrick's Heart Surgery and Lee's Superman Moment (McLaughlin family story)

Lee and I had been married for almost five years when Patrick was born. We already had one child, Timothy, who was twenty-two months old at Patrick's birth. At that time, I was an immature believer, and Lee was a nonbeliever. (He believed in God as a concept, but never started a relationship with Him. Lee considered himself to be self-sufficient and could not perceive a need for God.)

Patrick came along during a New Year's Eve party that Lee and I were hosting at our old farmhouse in Point Marion, Pennsylvania. It was just a small party including mostly family. Patrick was not due to be born for another two weeks, and there was no indication that he was coming early.

About 10:00 pm, as I was busy serving our guests, my water broke. Not a gush, but enough that I could tell Patrick was on his way. Lee and I left our guests and drove to the hospital, in Morgantown, West Virginia, leaving family to care for Tim. At that point, I had no contractions.

Because it was New Year's Eve, the nurses and Operating Room staff had to wait on one of my doctors who was at a party (as well as to call in another doctor from another practice). Two of the three doctors in my OB-GYN practice were at parties and were drinking. (I made the ones who came to do my delivery let me smell their breath for alcohol). They needed two doctors there because it would be a Caesarian-section.

Because I had a C-section previously, the doctor insisted that I have another one for this delivery. The surgery and Patrick's birth went well. Our Patrick was the first baby born in Monongalia County, West Virginia in 1978. (Baby and Mama got our pics in the paper for such an amazing feat.)

Patrick was a beautiful, happy baby, and Lee and I enjoyed having him in my room during most of my hospital stay. After three or four days, he developed jaundice (yellowish skin showing that he was building up bilirubin in his system). Baby Patrick had to go under the 'bili' light, but that is not unusual for breast-fed babies. The bilirubin light worked perfectly, and it looked like we might be able to go home ahead of the seven-day hospital stay that was normal for those days. On the fifth day, we got word that something was wrong with Patrick's heart.

That started a series of medical exams as they tried to discover what the problem was. Eventually, the doctors figured out that Patrick had a PDA, a Patent Ductus Arteriosus. For some reason, the small artery that causes blood to bypass the baby's lungs while it is in the womb, did not close off as it should have. This meant that a large part of Patrick's blood was bypassing his lungs and not getting oxygenated.

Patrick was a bluish, exhausted baby. He needed the repair surgery but was too small and delicate as a newborn. We had to wait, watch, and let him grow. This period was agony for Lee and me. It was also hard on our parents and family.

Patrick was a happy but rather small baby. He would fall asleep when he was nursing before he filled up his tummy, so he would nurse often. When he started crawling, he would have to stop and rest periodically because he would get so exhausted. Tim, who was still essentially a baby himself, loved his 'baby Paturck'. He would sit down to hold 'his baby' in his lap, but Mom or Dad had to be right there to catch Patrick when Tim decided he was done.

It was during this period that I started to spend more time with God, seeking comfort in the Bible and prayer. Honestly, in my prayer time, I spent as much time yelling at God as talking with him, but God seemed to have no problem with my honest interaction. I kept telling God that I did not want my baby to go through all of this— "please let it be me instead of him" was my fervent, repeated prayer.

Through all of this, God knew that I needed help in learning how to pray, so he arranged for our church to be having a study on the Lord's Prayer. The class taught how to use that model for deep, rich interaction with God. (Remember once again, there are no coincidences, only God-arrangements.) As I learned more about prayer, my dependence on God increased and my fear decreased. (Not that I was completely without fear, but at least I was less frantic.)

The doctors wanted to wait until Patrick was a year old to do his repair surgery. Unfortunately, the PDA was large, and it was spurting blood hard against the aorta. They worried that the force of the blood flow would cause damage to the aorta, so they scheduled his surgery for when he was ten months old instead of one-year old.

My mom, who was an amazing medical research librarian, found a pediatric cardiac surgeon, Dr. H, in Pittsburgh. He was among the top ten pediatric cardiac surgeons in the nation. Amazingly, he also turned out to

be a Christian. We told him that, as we entrusted our
beloved son into his hands, we were praying for his every
thought, word, and action. (Lee at this point was starting
to realize how much he needed God—more on that later).
Dr. H humbly thanked us, and the preparatory procedures
began at University of Pittsburgh Medical Center
Children's Hospital.

The first one of these invasive tests was a cardiac
catheterization. This procedure was done about two
weeks before the actual surgery was scheduled. Lee and I
were in the waiting room, nervously awaiting Patrick's
test to be finished. As we sweated it out, another couple
got news that their baby had a reaction to the dye injected
during the heart catheterization, and the baby died. Lee
and I suffered for them greatly, and our own fears
increased. You can believe that I was talking to God
bigtime and asking him to protect our precious Patrick.

In addition to praying for Patrick, my awareness of others
around us was greater because the Holy Spirit was
opening my eyes. I prayed for the bereaved parents who
lost their baby and the others in the waiting room.

There were also three kids in the waiting room, all grade
school age. There were no parents with them. I noticed
that they seemed very distraught, and I felt the Holy
Spirit's nudge to go talk to them. As I asked them about
why they were there, they poured out their story. Their
mom was still in the hospital after the birth of their baby
brother. She was having medical problems, and the kids
were worried sick about her. Their new baby brother was
getting his heart catherization right at that time. Their
poor dad was splitting his time going between the new
baby who was born with heart problems and his wife with
her medical issues. The kids were temporarily on their
own. These sweet children had pooled their money and
wanted to go to the gift shop to get their mom and baby

sibling each a gift. However, they were not allowed in the store without an adult. I got to be their adult! It was a privilege—it gave them help and comfort and gave me temporary distraction. They loved having me pray with them for their mom and baby brother. I don't know how things turned out for their family, but it was a sweet little God-gift to those kids and to me.

Finally, the day for the heart surgery arrived. They wheeled Patrick away from us on a gurney with him crying and reaching for us. It broke our hearts for this tiny person to have to go through such a big ordeal. The surgery would take a few hours, and I told Lee that I was going to the chapel to pray.

Lee, at that point, still had only his intellectual assent that God existed. He still resisted calling on Jesus and asking him to be his Savior and Lord. When I left him alone, it suddenly hit him like a ton of bricks that his beloved, small son was going under the knife. Lee could not stop it from happening; he could not help Patrick; and he was totally not in control. Lee urgently wanted to talk to God but did not want to go to the chapel with me.

My sweet Lee went into an old-fashioned red phone booth that was in the lobby. He picked up the phone and 'called God'. He turned his back to anyone who might see him through the phone booth glass. He cried out to God and told him that he no longer wanted to be self-sufficient. He wanted God in his life, in his heart and in control. In every way! He understood what Jesus did for him on the cross as a substitution for his personal sin. There, in that phone booth, Lee started his life as a new Christian. Lee called that his 'superman moment'. He went into the phone booth as Clark Kent and came out as Superman. Instead of wearing the superman outfit, he was wearing the righteousness of Jesus.

When Patrick's surgery was done, Dr. H told us it was a total success. We got to see our baby in ICU. It was a heartbreaking sight—Patrick seemed to have bandages and tubes everywhere. He could not make a noise because of the tube that had been in his throat. They told us to touch him, but it was hard to find any skin to touch.

The next day was totally different. Patrick was standing up and bouncing up and down in his hospital crib—they put a high cage type attachment on top so that he would not climb out. It was hard to believe that it was the same baby. Before he went home, he was going up and down the halls in a baby walker. Everyone he met would get a bright smile and a "hi". The nurses and all the staff would regularly come to see their 'miracle baby'. They needed the encouragement. Taking care of sick babies is hard and sometimes heartbreaking work.

This story does have a happy ending—a miracle ending. One day after the surgery, we bought Patrick a little T-shirt that said, "Jesus gave me my happy heart." Of course, this was true in two ways. Patrick has always had a sunny, joyful heart. The second way, of course, was that God totally restored Patrick's physical heart. When we took him back for his return appointment, the doc said, "He is done. You don't have to bring him back. No restrictions. He can be a Heisman trophy winner." (Patrick did give some serious effort to football but did not win the Heisman.)

Moreover, God does not do things halfway. I stayed with Patrick in the hospital while Lee tended the home fires as well as trying to limp along in his engineering job. At the hospital, God provided two old friends (who had moved to Pittsburgh) to encourage me, to give me guidance about Pittsburgh, and to be friendly faces. I just 'happened' to bump into them—they both worked at Children's. (Remember, no coincidences.)

Also, Lee and I were poor at that time of our lives. Lee was working, and I was not. We had bought an old farmhouse so had depleted our small savings. We had no money to pay for Patrick's surgery. UPMC contacted us about a program that was going on at the time for Pennsylvania residents. The program helped those whose residence was in PA with medical bills, depending on their income and some other factors. God, through the state of Pennsylvania, completely paid for every penny of Patrick's surgery.

Jesus truly did give Patrick his happy heart. Patrick's name means 'noble one". The biblical meaning of 'noble one' is a man of high integrity who is trustworthy.

Psalm 16:3. "I say of the holy people who are in the land, they are the noble ones in whom is all my delight."

Thank You, God, for our second beautiful boy. Thank You for bringing my wonderful Lee into the Kingdom. In Jesus' name, Amen

Kevin's Foot (McLaughlin family story)

In the year 2000, we took a trip to Europe. Tim was already married and had flown the coop. So, it was Lee, Patrick, Kevin, and me on our big adventure. It was a wonderful time, which we purposely left very loosely planned. We picked a general route, and we bought a bed and breakfast directory to find a daily place to stay, as needed. The planned length of the trip was to be two weeks long.

We rented the biggest SUV that we could find, which was small by American standards. It was a standard transmission—that was all we could get. Patrick ended up driving for two reasons. In the first place, he is an excellent driver, plus the driving was on the left-hand side of the road. It was easier for younger brain cells to adapt to that change, and Patrick had recently been a student in Europe for part of his university time, so he had done some left-side driving. (We started out with Lee driving and quickly learned that the reverse-side driving was a problem for him.)

Our first stay was in a Bed and Breakfast in the French countryside near Paris--our quarters were in a separate small building near our host's home. In the morning, we had a delicious breakfast with our hosts then went to pack up the car. While we were putting our luggage in the back end, Patrick was acclimating himself to the car so he could take over the driving. Somehow, during the familiarizing process, the car drifted back on top of Kevin's right foot. Before our yelling alerted Patrick, the car sat there for a few seconds.

Immediately after Patrick moved the car forward, I was on the ground with my hand on Kevin's foot praying, "Lord, please touch Kev's foot and heal it. Please don't let it be broken or injured." It was not a great or fancy prayer, just a plea for God's help.

At first, Kev couldn't tell us if there was damage or not because his foot was numb. As the numbness wore off, we waited to see if he was badly injured. He was not hurt at all! Not even bruised. Not a mark on him. Not a pain or twitch. We were able to complete our two-week trip. The four of us hiked, climbed hills, carried backpacks, and did anything we wanted to do without any problems.

Jeremiah 17:14 "Heal me, O Lord, and I shall be healed; save me, and I shall be saved, for you are my praise."

Another tender mercy and miracle from God! Thank You, Father. In Jesus' name, Amen

Israel Trip (McLaughlin family story)

Lee and I traveled to Israel with a group from our church. It was a fairly large number of people—we saw the sights by traveling on a large bus. Our pastor was an expert on Israel, because in addition to being a Bible and theology scholar, he was a student of history. Moreover, he had traveled to Israel a few times previously. Between our pastor and the tour bus driver, we had lots of expert guidance and commentary—spiritual, historical, and practical.

One thing both our tour guide and our minister tried to protect the group from was eating food that would make us sick. Unfortunately, almost at the end of the trip, we all ate at a market which apparently had some bad food. Almost the entire group got an intestinal bug with extreme cramping and diarrhea. I got the extreme cramping but for some reason, I could not move the bug through me. I could not pass anything at all but had a roiling painful war going on in my gut. While the rest of the group had the virus or infection pass through them quickly, I continued to suffer to the point that Lee and I were thinking of going to an emergency room in Israel.

Thankfully, I thought of Mary Hamrick, an amazing, faithful prayer warrior. The church had paid for her to go on the trip for her organizational skills, but also much more than that. Mary had a reputation as a woman of who prayed mightily.

I approached Mary and told her of my situation, asking her to pray for me. What she did reminded me of Elijah praying for the widow's son[24] or of Paul praying for Eutychus[25] (who went to sleep and fell from a window to his death while listening to Paul preach). Each time, these men of prayer lay completely against the body for whom they were praying. When I asked Mary to pray, we were standing in a parking lot with some others from our group. Others were already in the building where we were to eat dinner that evening. When starting her prayer, Mary completely flattened her body against mine with her arms around my shoulders. I was struck by her absolute lack of self-consciousness—this woman was only aware of the Holy Spirit and me. She prayed out loud, but quietly and with great authority. I don't remember the words.

Immediately, with Mary's prayer, the rumbling and pain in my intestines stopped. Remember the story of Jesus speaking to the storm, wind, and waves saying, "Peace, be still." (Mark 4:39) Afterwards, total calmness reigned. That is what happened in my body. Total chaos, inflammation, and pain, then complete and total peace. In one instant!

Just as a side note, someone else in the group who had the bug, asked Mary why she did not pray for her also. Mary said, "You did not ask me to pray." It reminded me of the verse, "You have not because you ask not."[26]

There was a last dinner planned for the group, which I thought I would be unable to eat. However, I did eat the final meal with the group. I felt totally fine and had no recurrence of symptoms on the trip.

Psalm 103:1-5. "Praise the Lord, my soul; all my inmost being, praise his holy name. Praise the Lord, my soul, and forget not all his benefits—who forgives all your sins and heals all your diseases, who redeems your life from the pit and crowns you with love and compassion, who satisfies your desires with good things, so that your youth is renewed like the eagle's."

Thank You, God, for putting people of great faith in our lives. Thank You for answering prayer, sometimes immediately and dramatically. In Jesus' name, Amen

Healed While Going (McLaughlin family story)

While cross country skiing in 2019, I had a fall and completely tore my left shoulder labrum. This structure is a cartilage lip that goes around the top of the socket where the head of the humerus (or upper arm bone) moves. The labrum also provides an attachment for various structures, one of which is the tendon to the long head of the biceps. The long head of my biceps was also partially torn from its attachment with my injury.

The labrum adds to shoulder stability by deepening the socket and aids in pain-free shoulder movement by preventing the head of the humerus from sliding up against the tendons and ligaments. After the tear, I not only had pain but lost significant function because my arm motions kept reinjuring the tendons and ligaments.

It was quite painful and despite my knowing how to treat it with ice and gentle range of motion exercise (because I am a physical therapist), I lost strength and range of motion. Sleeping was quite difficult also, for two reasons. The pain from the injury kept me awake, plus I am a sidesleeper and could no longer sleep on either side.

I tried babying and resting my shoulder, but that was not at all helpful. When all my interventions did not work, I finally saw an orthopedic doctor. He first recommended surgery, then retracted that course of action after hearing that I had previously had lymph nodes removed under the left arm because of breast cancer. (Trauma of any kind to an arm after having lymph nodes removed can cause lymphedema, a painful and function-limiting swelling caused by lymphatic fluid not being carried away properly. It is generally not reversible once it starts, hence the emphasis on prevention.)

At many times in my life, when I'm wanting God to do something, I just ask then look for him to do what I requested. Sometimes he does. However, from my experience, God often works differently. Frequently, it's a collaborative effort for the two of us together. God calls me to do something, and during my acting in obedience, God answers my prayer. As I obey, I see God's answer. Of course, he is the God of the Universe who does as he pleases—I cannot manipulate him with my actions or thoughts.

At any rate, as far as my shoulder, I was left with the only solution to my injury being prayer. Pray I did, but also, I was nudged by the Holy Spirit to start swimming laps. This started with very awkward left arm motions, as I attempted to do the crawl (free style). I kept at it day after day, ignoring the increase in pain. Gradually, my swimming stroke improved, and my number of laps increased until I could do a mile. At the end of a few months, I ended up with full range of motion, full strength, and zero pain. I can sleep on my left shoulder and fully use it without pain. Amazingly, I can even scratch the itchy spot on my back that requires great left shoulder flexibility. However, here is still one activity that I won't do—cross country ski!

Luke 17:14 "He (Jesus) looked at them and said, "Go to the Jewish priest and show him that you are healed!" And as they were going, their leprosy disappeared."

Thank You, God, for healing me as I went (obeyed your gentle nudge to swim), just as You healed the lepers as they walked in obedience to your command. In Jesus' name, Amen

Conclusions

The people involved in these miracles of healing blew me away. Betty constantly looked for ways to bless, pray for, and encourage others even when she was amidst her own suffering. She could have just hunkered down and focused on surviving. Because of hearing Betty's story, I now find myself constantly looking around for ways to bless and build others up.

The willingness of each of these persons to take the next steps (as they were guided into them) also stood out to me. They did not just sit back and do nothing. These miracles involved a high level of cooperation and active participation. Could this be why so many of these episodes caused great growth and maturing of the people involved?

Another gem that I discerned was the acceptance of tough things by these individuals. Betty did not rail against God because her liver failed. Sarah and Preston lost a child, but instead of ruminating on what they lost-- they look forward to a heavenly reunion. To a person, you see trust and obedience without bitterness or anger.

Another hero whom I took note of was Darryl, who has now gone home to the Lord. Instead of viewing his extension of life as a gift for him and his family, he looked for the deeper purpose. His bonus time was not for his own goals but rather to tell people of God's love and mercy.

Miracles of healing are all around us. Do we see them? Are we grateful for them? These stories have opened my eyes not only to see healing miracles, but also to perceive how we can grow because of our suffering. We can let opportunities slip by to cooperate with God as he builds our character in the experiences of suffering.

Amazingly, we can also use these times to learn to live life more like Jesus did

Questions to ponder:

1. Have you seen God's hand in healing you or someone you love? Can you relate a story?
2. Do you think it is a miracle when someone is healed if the medical system is part of the process?
3. Does it hurt your faith in God because he does not heal everyone? Can you share how you feel about this honestly and respectfully?

CHAPTER 4--MIRACLES OF PROVISION

It is so easy to overlook these miracles because God constantly provides for all of us in every moment. Soak in these provision stories then open your eyes to the many ways that God gives to you personally. Develop a grateful heart like the individuals in the stories that you are about to read.

A Way Out

Did you ever hear a story that broke your heart but gave you hope at the same time? My friend, Francie, has lived such a tale, and it has left her with a catchphrase that resounds in her heart. She shortens it to 'TNO'. Trust No One! (Interestingly, the Bible says something similar about Jesus. He would not entrust himself to people because he knew their hearts.[27])

Oddly enough, despite the heartbreak of her life (beginning in her earliest years), Francie exudes trust and courage. She chooses to live fully, to love wholeheartedly, and to invest herself in others again and again.

Francie has been an enigma to me from the beginning of our relationship, which started in 1974, when my first job as a home health physical therapist intersected with hers as a home health nurse. As a relatively new, but very ignorant Christian, my knowledge of Francie did not fit into my simplistic worldview, because her love of others was more real, active, and tangible than mine or that of most Christians that I knew. Francie, by her own account, is not a Christian.

Because she was always so grounded and well put together, I never suspected the heartbreak that has checkered Francie's life. Her early birthday memories include listening to a repeated recitation of her Father's disappointment in having three girls. Francie was the third girl born into a family where she was repeatedly told that only boys were valued. "I remember when you were born, Francie. That's when I knew that I was a three-time loser," was her dad's repeated mantra on every birthday.

Her childhood was also shadowed by neglect and poverty because her college-educated parents refused to work to provide for her family. The basic needs were not met for these daughters, especially their need for love and affirmation. The betrayal of her neglectful parents continued to reverberate in her life, as the open wound in her heart seemed to attract more treacheries to come, each one worse than the last. (These will not be addressed in this story—it would take a whole book to describe them, which Francie is now in the process of writing.)

Francie grew up in a small coal mining town in Pennsylvania which appeared to have a dark pall over it, spiritually as well as physically, (with coal dust overshadowing and permeating everything). It was a place filled with bigotry and hopelessness along with some shining spots of light here and there. This story is about one of those glistening spots of light that enabled Francie to escape the dark, dreary life in a small town that had lost its sense of hope and wonder.

Francie always stood out academically and in every other way. As a tall, thin, brunette with lots of drive and ability, she was a shining star. Not only was Francie gifted, but she has also always been real, relatable, and caring. Like a flower blooming in a crack of a stone wall, Francie persevered all through her childhood. Optimism and humor have always been her hallmarks.

As Francie neared the end of high school, hard circumstances took her to a dark place. Her long-time boyfriend was killed in a mining catastrophe.

Francie applied to a nearby nursing school and was miraculously accepted, even though she knew that her family could not afford four years of college tuition. However, the program that Francie selected was only six hundred and fifty dollars, total. This program was comprised of three years of year-round school that would give Francie a diploma as a Registered Nurse.

Right before she was to start nursing school, Francie's mother told her their family could not afford to pay her way (even though her parents always managed to have money for beer and cigarettes). Francie would not be allowed to attend.

She was reeling from the disappointment when she got a call on the weekend before classes were to begin (on Monday). A women's organization in a small town nearby had somehow heard of Francie's need, and they wanted to loan her the money to go to nursing school. Francie accepted.

While in Nursing School, her best friend lost her life in a freak accident. (She was swimming in the river when a barge on the waterway turned on its engine and sucked her into the turbine.) Francie was left thinking that she was a pariah—everyone whom she loved would be destroyed. It was a gloomy period in her life, but she did what she always did--she moved forward.

Francie finished the grueling program and became an excellent nurse. Yet, she is so much more than a nurse— an entrepreneur, a business starter, an administrator, an avid volunteer, an excellent leader, and a motivator. I know firsthand of her exceptional abilities—she later became my boss at a home health agency that she began and ran.

Surprisingly, Francie will agree that the provision of the money for nursing school was a miracle, even though she classifies herself as a non-Christian. (It is my own cherished belief that Francie will soon fully embrace Jesus.)

It is hard for all of us when we go through extreme suffering to imagine that a good Lord could allow these things to happen. Because God gives human beings the right to make choices, it opens the door for horrible things to occur. Yet, those terrible happenings can somehow be redeemed in ways we cannot see. And our loving God is there with us through it all, hurting as we do (even before we start a relationship with Him).

Because of her selfish earthly parents and other sad events, a loving and nurturing heavenly Father is not someone Francie can comprehend or embrace. It is hard for her to picture a Father who lovingly watches over and provides for his children, because her parents did not do

that, and other tragedies followed her. Yet, I know of her
constant drive to know the truth, to grow into all that she
can be, and to love and be loved. I am confident that she
will seek Him, and He will find her.

John 14:27 "I am leaving you with a gift—peace of mind
and heart. And the peace I give is a gift the world cannot
give. So don't be troubled or afraid."

Father, thank You for your provision of the tenderhearted women who lent Francie the money to go to
nursing school. I don't understand why such hard
circumstances happen to anyone, but maybe those things
helped to shape her into the amazing woman that she is
now. It is astonishing that she has held onto her kind and
giving heart. Please complete what You have started in
her loving soul and help her to know Your tender care for
her.
In Jesus name, Amen

A Simple Miracle with Ripple Effects

Dr. John E. Sneckenberger (Ed) was one of Lee's
engineering professors at West Virginia University. Lee
loved him in college and in many ways modeled himself
after 'Sneck' (Lee's affectionate name for Dr.
Sneckenberger). Sneck was a good mentor for Lee as an
engineer but also in how to live life as a Christian man,
husband, and father. His wife, Scottie, has also been an
example to us. Both are always full of joy,
encouragement, and godly wisdom. I know that Lee has
also always admired Sneck's thirst for knowledge, his
open-mindedness to better ways of doing things, and his
worldview (which has always been colored with a little
humor).

Recently, Lee dropped by to visit his professor/mentor, and he told him that I was writing this book. Dr. Sneckenberger told Lee about a miracle that positively affected his life. (I believe that it has touched other lives also through ripple effects.)

In their younger days when their three daughters were about seven, ten, and twelve years-old, respectively, Ed and Scottie went to his parent's house near Greencastle, Pennsylvania. Ed's mom had recently died, leaving the old homestead empty. Of his four siblings, Ed was geographically the closest to his parent's home, therefore the maintenance of the property fell on him until they collectively decided what to do with it. From the Sneckenberger's home in Morgantown, West Virginia, it took about four hours to drive there.

One weekend, the family made the jaunt to do yardwork and cleaning, with the whole family working together to get it done. It came to Sunday evening and time to make the four-hour drive home (because the girls had school the next morning). Sneck could not find the car keys, which were also on the same key ring as their house key in Morgantown. Scottie could not find a back-up key either. First, Ed searched alone, retracing his footsteps. Next, the whole family joined in, as the time got later, and the drive home loomed ahead of them.

Finally, Sneck got frustrated, a little panicked, and started talking to God, "Lord, we need those keys!" He got the definite impulse to walk back to the back fence and look in the lawn. The prompting led him to exactly the right place to look down and see the keys nestled in the grass.

This miracle had a profound effect on Ed and probably the whole family. Even more so, it was a gift that keeps on giving. Here is what our wise professor says about this and other miracles, "We are able to believe in God because every day is a miracle from the Lord. When we have a real need and a miracle happens, it makes God more real in our lives. It also gives us a reason to explain God to others."

Did you catch that? The ripple effects! As these miracles happen to Ed, he uses them to talk about God to others.

Sneck does not believe that miracles alone are enough to keep us moving forward towards God and into his purposes for us. As a young man, he began memorizing Bible verses starting with John 3:16. In addition to helping Sneck to know God better, these verses have given him a basis for telling people about the Lord when they ask. "Those verses become a part of us—we live with them. They help when people want to know about God."

Another thing that helped Ed was to have a definite understanding of the time when he became part of the Kingdom of God. Knowing for certain that you are God's child is foundational to life with Christ. It also gives a basis to share with others.

To quote Ed, "There is always a reason to say, 'Yes, I do believe in God.' Seeing God answer prayers is a joy for the rest of your life."

John 3:16 "For God so loved the world that he gave his one and only Son, that whoever believes in him shall not perish but have eternal life."

Father, thank You for mentors and positive examples that You put into our lives. Thank You for the ripples that affect other lives in countless helpful ways. Thank You for this gentle and kind man and for the ways that he has aided others in their journey to know and love You. In Jesus' name, Amen

A Working Man

A long-term friend of ours, whom I will call George (not his real name), told me this story. It happened around October of 1985 in West Virginia. He had worked in the city of Wheeling, West Virginia, at Wheeling Machine until its recent closure. Despite all-out effort, George could not find local work, and he used up his unemployment benefits. He had many skills as a handyman, but those were extremely tough times. George refused to sign up for welfare—that was something he just would not do.

George, his wife, and his two young sons did all they could to cut back on expenses. With his hunting ability, George kept wild game on the table. He also kept the freezer full of deer meat so he could be sure that his family would not go hungry. Despite all their efforts, the money dwindled until the only bill on which they were current was their electric bill. Their water and gas had been turned off for non-payment. The mortgage payment was three months in arrears--the bank was threatening to claim ownership of their home.

Finally, George heard of a framing job in New Jersey-- he was hired to run the telescopic boom. He rode with his boss and a few others in his boss's truck. There was no room in the front of the truck, so George wore a snowmobile suit and curled his body into a frozen, huddled ball in the open back of the truck for the eight hour drive. (He did this each time they made this trek.)

While he was gone, George told his family to keep warm in the smallest bedroom with an electric space heater because the weather was starting to turn cold. His wife and sons went to George's mom's house nearby to shower and fill up jugs of water. They still had plenty of deer meat thanks to George's hunting. Surprisingly, the family did not seem to be traumatized or worried about any of this. They viewed it like an adventure, a camping trip of sorts.

Meanwhile, in New Jersey, George worked extremely hard. He drove the big piece of machinery (the boom), but he also drove nails, or did whatever was needed. He economized in every way possible so that every penny could go towards his family's needs. He and the crew camped out in a cheap rental beach house, using sleeping bags on the floor. On his first trip back home, George had made enough to pay the utility bills and the three months mortgage payment to get caught up. The miracle was not only that he made the money that was needed, but also that he got back with the necessary payments with one day to spare. To get the mortgage paid before his house would be repossessed, he had to drive the check from Wheeling, West Virginia, to Charleston. He made it just in the nick of time.

After three months of traveling back and forth to work in New Jersey, George was able to find a local job. He chuckles when he remembers the story because he loves how God does things. He is convinced that many times God waits until the very last minute to answer prayers for one reason--God wants to grow and stretch us. He wants to build our trust and faith. Our heavenly Father wants us to become more like Jesus in character, so he lets us have these big challenges and narrow escapes.

George had many more stories, like this one, of periods when he had to travel, sleep in the front seat of his truck (sharing his space with the manual gear shift) and do many difficult jobs to provide for his family. George did not see that as a hardship or burden—he just saw it as doing what needed to be done.

This story is a miracle in two ways. George had to sacrifice greatly for his part to make sure his wife and sons had what they needed—the Holy Spirit in George compelled him to do these right things. (Without the power of the Holy Spirit, we are motivated to survive and care only for ourselves. The ability to sacrifice is a miraculous change imbued on us by the Helper.) As George was daily in the trenches, doing what had to be done, God was right there encouraging and empowering him.

The other miracle, as I see it, is the love that God puts into a believing man for his spouse and children. He will do whatever it takes to provide for and to protect them. It brings tears to my eyes to see the character that God put into real men to care for their families. They do it with joy and without complaint. I am in awe of them.

1 Timothy 5:8. "But if anyone does not provide for his relatives, and especially for members of his household, he has denied the faith and is worse than an unbeliever."

Father, thank You, for the hearts that you put into real men. Men who love and serve their families. Men who do what it takes. Thanks also, for Your provision. In Jesus' name, Amen

The House Whisperer

June and Bill Straub were living on Bill's family farm when a coal company approached them and told them they would be mining under their farm and home. (In West Virginia, the surface rights and mineral rights can belong to different owners.) The likelihood of damage to the house was high, and they were offered options before the mining started. Their possible choices were to sell the house and property to the mining company, to take a settlement before mining commenced and keep the house, or to wait and see what damage was done and rely on the coal company to fix it adequately. (I won't keep you in suspense--it did turn out that their house was subsequently greatly damaged by the mining.)

To understand the trauma of this whole process, know that Bill's family had been on this farm since the revolutionary war. Bill and June did not want to move— they loved where they lived. Bill's hobby was carpentry, and he had invested much of himself in their home, the old barn (where he did his woodworking projects), and the twenty six-and one-half acres of land surrounding them.

During this period, June spent many wakeful hours at night having conversations with God. Bill and June started looking at houses and property and could not find anything at all. (June told Bill that she would go door to door to places she liked and start asking if they were thinking of selling. This thought horrified Bill, but June asked him what homeowner would not be complimented by that.) There was a deadline looming over them with no solutions in sight.

June would awaken at night, praying and reading inspirational stories. Although she was very unsettled, during one of her prayer times she had a vision of Jesus holding a girl with dark curly hair (herself as a child). She began praying with peace and confidence that God would send them exactly where He wanted them to be. "I am your daughter, and You know me," she told Him in complete trust. She also told her heavenly Father, "I want my own story to tell—I want to tell of your goodness!"

The problem was not just finding a new home but also letting go emotionally of their homeplace. Finally, they came up with a partial solution and proposed it to the coal company. They would sell the house and two-and one-half acres around it—but they would keep the rest of the property. Miraculously, the coal company agreed to do this for the same offered price for the whole property.

Of course, that still left the problem of needing a place in which to move. June thought of the area of Wheeling that she enjoyed most--her favorite place was the Chapel Hill area. June and Bill had some friends who lived on Chapel Hill Road, and they approached them to ask them if they knew of any property for sale. They explained their dilemma of wanting one to five acres of land on which to build, and the four of them spent three hours discussing it. While this couple was sympathetic, they had no solutions.

However, the next day when June called her friends to thank them, their friends said they should get together to discuss the problem again. This couple owned four acres and they were willing to talk to Bill and June about selling them some land. They had never had good friends in such a dilemma, and they wanted to help. The two couples worked out the details in person, and the upshot was that Bill and June gained a spectacular two-and-seven-tenths acres on which they built a lovely new home. The view and sunsets from their back porch are beyond gorgeous, and the neighbors on each side are the kind that we all wish to have. (Right now, as Bill is laid up after a horrible bicycling accident, the neighbors compete to be the ones to mow their lawn for them.)

However, June's function as House Whisperer was not finished. She saw a need and started up her focused nighttime prayers again. Bill and June's family is a blended family, with his kids and her kids, who are all adults now. Bill has a daughter with multiple sclerosis who, at that time, lived in a house totally unsuited to her growing unsteadiness. Her home was unsafe for her to get

around with a cane. The house was multiple stories with a
bathroom on the second floor and one in the basement,
but none on the first floor. (As a result, she tried not to
drink much water during the day because of her difficulty
navigating the steps.) June was concerned for her
stepdaughter and began praying proactively. Her prayer
was, "God send her where you want her to be."

June and Bill started watching for suitable property to
come on the market. June told Bill that because of the
dearth of good properties on the market, they needed to
be ready for when a good prospect became available.
They got a home equity loan in place so that if the right
house showed up, they could jump on it.

One morning, June was looking at the Realtor.com
website and saw a one-story house that just came on the
market. She told Bill, and they immediately drove there
to look at it without an appointment. They drove slowly
by and saw a woman working in the yard. They kept
driving by to scope it out, until they could tell that the
woman was curious about their scrutiny.

They stopped to talk to the lady and discovered that it had
been her parent's home. She and her sister were selling it
after their father's recent death. It was a 1950's home
which had been under contract, but the buyers had not
come through with the money in the allotted time. The
owner told June that she was faced with the decision of
whether to renew the contract with the previous buyers by
4:00 pm that afternoon.

This gracious lady gave June and Bill a tour of the house.
They could easily see that, despite being outdated and
having a totally gutted bathroom, it had good bones
(including the original hardwood floors). Bill could use
his carpentry skills to make it a great home for his
daughter. Before the day was out, there was a handshake

deal with a five-hundred-dollar deposit to hold the property. It also turned out that the realtor who had listed the property had lapsed in time on his sales contract, so Bill and June's realtor-friend helped with all the details of the transaction. They also knew a trusted lawyer to do the required title searches. Everything that was needed was there to make this house sale happen. Bill's daughter checked out the property the next day, and, with all the details already in place, the deal went through.

The guys in Bill's bicycling group, as well as other friends, showed up every day to work on the house. They added grab bars, railings, a handicapped-accessible bathroom, and made the home totally functional for Bill's daughter. Bill told June that they needed all-new kitchen cabinets, but June reconfigured the cabinets and Bill added some custom ones that he built so that his daughter could easily move around in the kitchen safely. When they were finished with the home, it was cute and perfect for someone with decreased strength and balance.

June waited until Bill's daughter was in the home for some time before she told her the story of how God had put this all together for her. She wanted her stepdaughter to experience how completely suited the home was for her before she heard the House-Whisperer tale.

June is one of those people whom you love to be around because she is joyful and radiant. Whenever I see her, I always say to myself, "The party can start now, because June is here!"

Despite many difficult things that have come into her life, June says, "God gives to me, and gives to me, and gives to me!" I asked her to define a miracle, and here is what she said, "If you believe in God, and you quiet the chaos in your mind when tough things happen, then you can see

God's hand in everything. That is a miracle! A miracle is when God makes his presence known."

Psalm 37:23 "The Lord directs the steps of the godly. He delights in every detail of their lives."

Father, thank You for the example of one of your children living in such joy and simple trust. Help us all to grow into such a childlike love of You. In Jesus' name, Amen

Gary and the Mercy Ship

My brother, Gary, as a recent graduate from medical school got to realize one of his goals. A dream that he had, from the time that he knew that he would be a doctor, was to practice medicine on a mission trip (or even possibly longer term). His first trip as a missionary doctor was a six-week stint on a Mercy Ship, which is a floating hospital that travels from port to port giving medical treatment to those who need it.

Among the mission workers, there were many young people in their twenties and thirties, and Gary grew close with a group of them. When it came time for one young man's mission interval to end, he needed a ride to the airport. The fun-loving group of friends decided they should all tag along for an adventure. Nine individuals piled into a small Fiat to drop this guy off.

All went well on the drive to the airport, and the group left their fellow worker to catch his flight. However, on the way back to the ship, a policeman pulled them over, speaking rapid Spanish, which Gary could not understand. Others in the car grasped his meaning--the upshot of the traffic stop was that they were ticketed for having too many people in the car. They were not allowed to go any farther--they had to get out, along an eight-lane highway in the middle of nowhere and find their way back to the ship.

This was much easier said than done. Next to the berm, blocking their view, was a tall wall over which they could not see. Boosting the lightest person onto shoulders, they discovered only fruit trees on the other side. There were no houses or businesses within sight. Walking all the way was unrealistic because they were quite a distance from the ship.

Everyone stuck out their thumbs to hitchhike a ride, but no passing cars even slowed down. The problem may have been the busy road, where it was dangerous to stop, plus the fact that they had eight people.

One in the group spoke up, "Look! What are we doing? We are from the Mercy Ship, for heaven's sake. We should pray!"

They gathered close to the wall, as far from traffic as they could get, and began praying. They did it with open eyes because of the heavy traffic. As they were finishing their prayer, they watched a small truck begin to cross all the way across four lanes of traffic in one swift move to reach the berm where they were standing. He pulled up to them just as they wrapped up their prayer.

They all piled into the back, and this good Samaritan gave them the ride they needed to the Mercy Ship. It was a small miracle as well as a reminder to ask God for help when we need it.

James 4: 2b "You do not have because you do not ask God."

Thank You, Lord, for providing for us when we call upon You. In Jesus' name, Amen

Angels in the French Countryside (McLaughlin family story)

When Patrick was in college and Kevin was a senior in high school, we took a trip to France. On our trip, the car that we rented, unbeknownst to us, had a diesel engine. No one told us this at the rental car place, so we just assumed that it was gas-powered. About the fourth or fifth day into our trip, we went out into the French countryside on a Sunday. Apparently, the region observed a Sunday rest, so nothing was open, but we stopped anyway at a small vineyard with a winery. Patrick sweettalked the owner into giving us a tour and wine-tasting all by ourselves. The man only spoke French, so the interaction was mostly between Patrick and the proud grape-grower/vintner, but we all felt his gentle spirit. The kindness of this man was exceptional—he made us feel special and warmly welcomed. (This was in stark contrast to the interactions we had been having with Paris citizens, which left us feeling like pond scum.) It was a lovely time, and we left in the late afternoon to find our next bed and breakfast from our little guidebook.

We had filled the rental car with gas at a self-service station before getting out into the rural area and had noticed some knocking in the engine throughout our ride. We thought maybe we put in the wrong grade of gasoline. After our visit to the winery, the car seriously started making noise then stopped dead as we pulled off the road to check it.

We had no choice but to get out and walk towards the next small village, which was about three miles away. (We did not have working cell phones in that area.) In hopes of finding a place to stay, we took our backpack-luggage with us. It was early evening by this time, and the only traffic was heading back towards Paris. We were walking the opposite way of passing cars on a narrow two-lane road without much in the way of berms. Lee headed our single-file row of walkers, with Patrick and Kev in the middle, and me in the back. Lee had reflective strips on his jacket sleeves and every time a car would approach, he would flash one towards the driver's headlights so he would see us.

We tried stopping at a home out in the country with no luck. As we continued walking, it started raining, so we were all colder and more miserable by the minute. As we walked, we noticed that only the dairy cows were with us out in this weather. We had no car; there was no place to stay; we were cold and hungry; and there seemed to be no way out of our dilemma. Bringing up the rear in our string of drenched wayfarers, I was softly praying out loud and constantly. The others did not say much—they just plodded along soggily. During our cold, wet and increasingly dark walk, primarily on my mind and heart was the fact that we had already had one miracle on the trip (Kevin's foot being healed), and I was totally expecting another. While being physically in discomfort, in my spirit, I was almost excited to see what God would do.

We finally reached the small village, and by this time it was full-on dark and very cold. The village was buttoned up tight. It was about 10:00 pm by this time, and there were not many lights on, even in the homes. Miraculously, we came upon a tavern that was somewhat lit-up. It had a 'Closed' sign up on the door, but we knocked anyway. We kept knocking until finally a woman came to the door to tell us they were closed. She spoke only French, and Patrick launched into telling our sad situation in her language. At first, she seemed somewhat hostile and suspicious. (We may have gotten her out of bed--it looked like she lived above the tavern.)

As Patrick spoke to her, her expression softened, and all at once, she took pity on us and invited us in.

She took charge of the whole situation after conferring with Patrick some more. She called our rental company. My paltry French was not good enough to understand what she said to the rental car agency, but she seemed to be chastising them (as if it was all their fault and not ours). Patrick later told us that she vigorously insisted that the agency take care of us immediately, leaving no doubt that the fault was all theirs.

We all bundled into a booth, and this kind woman rustled up some hot soup and bread to feed us. As we all started to warm up and get comfortable, we settled down to wait on a tow truck to come from the rental company. Our tavern-owner/advocate left us alone in our booth but made sure we had all we needed. We huddled together and hung out until the tow truck driver finally arrived close to midnight. We thanked the woman profusely and tried to give her money for all she had done for us. She categorically refused any payment.

We set off with another 'French-speaking-only' citizen in the tow truck from the rental agency—this man had stopped and loaded our rental car on his way to pick us up. Patrick sat in the front seat with our French mechanic, speaking in French to him, and the rest of us huddled sleepily in the back. In the next sequence of events, Patrick communicated our whole story; this gentleman dropped us at an inexpensive but comfy motel; and he told us that we would be picked up in the morning.

The next morning, the agency sent a car to get us. When we arrived at the dealership, the general manager greeted us. As we walked back to the service department, he told us that when he came in, he found our mechanic hard at work on our rental car. He informed us that our angel mechanic stayed up all night fixing our car. This amazing technician came over to us and presented us with a totally functional car. No blame on us, no complaints whatsoever, and no expectation of anything. He also, like the tavern owner, refused any money and sent us on our way. Even the manager of the dealership emphasized that this was all from the largesse of mechanic's heart. His all out, over-the-top service was a gift to us, and we owed him nothing.

We all felt certain that we had just been in the presence of some French-speaking angels (a vintner, a tavern owner, and a mechanic).

Galatians 6:2. Bear one another's burdens, and so fulfill the law of Christ.

Thank You, Lord, for the overwhelming kindness of strangers and for Your miracles when we are most in need. In Jesus' name, Amen

Cooking for a Mission Trip (McLaughlin family story)

I met one of my very best friends, at a prayer time in another friend's home. Gail blew my socks off with her faith, and I was drawn to her immediately. We had one prayer session together, then she invited me to be part of the cooking team with her and another friend of hers, Terry, for a mission trip to Mexico.

At this point in my life, I was anything but a good cook. Our family ate out for many meals, and the meals that we ate at home were often delivered pizza. Despite this fact, I took the matter of going on this trip to God in prayer. The Holy Spirit most definitely gave me a nudge to say yes, so the three of us set off on our adventure along with a group of about thirty high school students, a couple of other adult chaperones, plus the youth pastor.

As you get to know God, you see his sense of humor. Gail, Terry, and I were called to be the cooking team, and not one of us were cooks. Gail, however, was a master of microwaving. This was an important detail, as you soon will see.

We stayed on the campus of a ministry center in Mexico. An American couple had founded the mission. They had hopes to use it for helping youth in Mexico and wanted it to function as a training center and serving ground for American teens who desired to minister.

The project, in which we were to assist, was building a new dormitory. The team consisted of juniors and seniors from high school of both sexes, the adults who supervised the building (plus kept the teen angst under control), the youth minister, and our cooking trio. Two of the high school team members were Kevin, my son, and Brett, Gail's son.

The project was daunting, but for the most part the kids loved it. Sleeping and bathroom conditions were primitive, except for the kitchen, which had all the modern conveniences. That is where the cooking team lived and functioned. There was, however, no air conditioning anywhere, and the heat was brutal.

We soon learned that our function on this mission was not mainly as cooks--we were mediocre at best with our cooking. (We managed to make a Texas brisket taste like cardboard.) The kids were fed and had the basic nutrients they needed for sustenance with our cooking skills. (I guess another miracle is that nobody complained about the food.) However, it turned out that our main purpose on this mission was to be prayer warriors.

The kitchen quickly became the place that both the kids and the adults came when anything went sideways. A kid with a minor hurt, tempers that flared, relationships

which suffered, even needs for materials or finances—
nothing was too small or too large for prayer. For
anything or everything, members of the mission team
showed up at the kitchen, and we prayed. We had group
prayer in the mornings along with a huge group hug
before they started their work.

To further illustrate God's sense of humor and his
attention to detail, Gail's mastery of microwaving came
into play. Early in the trip, the main oven stopped
working. We had to prepare everything in the microwave.
Can you imagine feeding about forty people with just a
microwave? Because of Gail's skill, we fed the group
without a working oven. She stayed perfectly calm as she
guided our team to get meals on the table.

Things did go wrong. We thought one boy fractured his
foot. It was too hot for good sleep for anyone, and
tempers got short. Of course, there were also normal
construction challenges. However, it was a beautiful time
of seeing God care for his children, in all things big and
small.

Philippians 4:6 "Be anxious for nothing, but in everything
by prayer and supplication, with thanksgiving, let your
requests be made known to God."

It was a time of miracles. Thank You, God. In Jesus'
name, Amen

Conclusions

Miracles of provision often go unnoticed because God is
a good Father, who gives to us as part of his nature. Yet,
taking God's blessings for granted is what we do as His
children.

In these stories, provision was not taken for granted. Dr. Sneckenberger knew that God answered his prayer to find his keys, and he viewed it as an opportunity to tell others about God. June not only gives God credit for providing a new home, but she used her skills and intercession to make sure her stepdaughter was in a good house also.

Is prayer a part of getting provision? Yes, it can be. However, sometimes difficult, obedient steps are needed to follow through--like George working extremely hard to make sure his family was without need.

God takes delight in providing for the needs of his children, and sometimes he does it in miraculous ways. Often, He uses other people to provide like the truck driver who pulled across all the lanes of traffic to pick up the stranded Mercy Ship passengers, the mechanic who stayed up all night to fix our rental car, and the women's organization that loaned Francie money for nursing school.

Who are God's children? We are all made in his image, even though it is blurred by the sinfulness of the world. God desires to take us all under his wing of protection and provision. The Bible says that "In Him, we live and move and have our being."[28] That refers to all of us. Does he love us all? Without a doubt. Do we all love him back? No, we must accept His gift of love and sacrifice to be able to return His love.

My questions to myself in response to these stories are: "Do I give thanks for God's provisions?", and "Am I looking for ways that I can be part of those provisions to others?"

Questions to ponder:

1. Do you feel that it is fair to say that God gives us so much that we take it for granted and no longer perceive his provision? Can you reexamine your life to see the times when God has been part of the story?
2. How do we avoid the common pitfall of not having gratitude?
3. Have you considered keeping a gratitude journal? Could actively seeking ways to be thankful keep us from an attitude of entitlement?
4. Can you share a story of God's provision?

CHAPTER 5--THE MIRACLES OF NON-COINCIDENCES

There are amazing things that God puts together for us. We may choose to write those off as coincidences or open our eyes to see how those events are hand-crafted by God. Look for those miraculous non-coincidences in these stories.

Smog (McLaughlin family story)

This was a miracle within a miracle—it was contained inside the same time period as the miracle of Patrick's heart surgery. During the time before and around his surgery, I took a course in praying, based on the Lord's Prayer. Each line of the Lord's Prayer was expanded and explained in this course, then we were to put it into practice in our lives. This exercise was extremely faith building, because as you pondered the deep meanings of each part of Jesus' prayer example, you began to see how the Lord's Prayer is powerful and limitless. When we pray, we communicate to the one who spoke everything into being and who sustains it with just a word.

Each line of the prayer is important. The first line, "Our Father who art in heaven", puts us positionally where we should be. When you had a good and loving earthly father, like I did, this part is easy. Because I had a great father, I knew God is good, and I knew that as an

infinitely kind father, God loves me and protects me. (In ignorance, I assumed that good fathers are the norm. Unfortunately, this assumption does not seem to be true—
I have met so many wounded daughters and sons. Know and understand, my friend, that the deep wounds left by bad parenting or absence of nurturing can be healed. I pray that this healing comes to pass for you. Check out Elijah House International to find help.)

The next line, "Hallowed be thy name", puts our hearts in the place of awe and holy respect as we come before the King of Kings and Lord of Lords. Understanding the nature of God is a lifelong process (and beyond). Just rehearsing the characteristics of God's personality begins to build our ability to worship in spirit and in truth. This means that we begin to understand and appreciate the worth of our holy God. Going through the alphabet and thinking of a characteristic of God for each letter is an exercise that has helped me through the years. At times when I cannot pray, doing this practice has been a bridge of remembrance for me--recalling who God is and knowing He never changes.

"Thy Kingdom come." Where is God's kingdom? It can be here and now, as well as in heaven. C.S. Lewis said that we live in 'enemy-occupied territory', which is true. Adam gave over dominion of earth to Satan with his choice of disobedience. Yet, each of us can choose to let God's Kingdom live inside of us. We can choose Jesus and accept his gift of sacrifice and love. The Holy Spirit can reside in us and make us a part of the kingdom of heaven. Then with prayer and obedience, we can take back territory and expand God's kingdom around us. We can choose to live in the intersection between heaven and earth.

The next line is an important part of prayer— "Thy will be done, on earth as it is in heaven". How do we know God's will? How do we bring God's will to earth like it is in heaven? So simple. Ask Him! Then wait with open spiritual eyes and ears. Be attuned to his speaking to you from the Bible. A wise friend might talk to you about the very thing in which you have been seeking guidance, or events may pop up in your life that give you clear answers. Trust that if you ask God, you will get an answer. 'Yes, no, or wait.'

The next line is the part that most of us are good at doing. It is the asking part— "Give us this day our daily bread." Probably not many of us need training in asking God for what we want. The key part of this is that true prayer will adjust as we listen to God. We may start out with one prayer, but as we discern through the Spirit what God wants, we change our prayer to adapt to that. Prayers that change the world are the prayers that God plants in our hearts. Another part of supplication is noticing God's answers, being thankful about, and remembering all the ways that God has responded to our prayers. We become what we rehearse over and over. If we have thankful hearts, grateful for big and small miracles, we can become expectant, passionate people of peace, joy, and hope.

"And forgive us our trespasses as we forgive those who trespass against us." In this little sentence is the key to healing so many wounds and sins. This line, put into practice, could probably do away with most counseling and psychiatric practices. We all sin; we all hurt each other; and we must all ask for and accept forgiveness for deep healing at a heart-level to occur. Forgiveness for our sins is not completely accomplished until we also can truly forgive (not forget or excuse) the wounds and sins inflicted upon us. If we cannot forgive, then a root of bitterness will grow and take over our heart, leaving us with hatred, anger, and confusion. Understand that a component of forgiveness is our choice, and another part of it is divine, a gift from God to accomplish what we cannot completely do on our own.

The next line is a sad commentary on the reality of living in a fallen world. "And lead us not into temptation but deliver us from evil." Even the best of us cannot live without sinning. Non-Christians and Christians both disobey God. It is our human condition, brought upon everyone with the choice of Adam and Eve to disobey. However, (with the help of God, as we ask and seek to obey) we can grow in our ability to hear, follow God, and sin less and less. When we mess up; when we hurt another; when we are selfish and self-seeking; we have an advocate with the Father. This defender/ champion /supporter is Jesus who experienced everything that we do. He sits on the right of the Father and talks to God about our sins. I can hear him saying, "Father-God, she is trying. She did not mean to be thoughtless and careless of those around her. Please pick her up God, wash off her heart so that it does not stay dirty and get hardened. Please show her how to do better next time. Forgive her, Father."

"For thine is the kingdom, the power and the glory forever." When we recognize who is the King of all creation, the source of all power, and the one to whom all glory belongs, it readjusts our thinking and priorities. It helps us to know that He is the Majesty, and we are subject to Him. Our main purpose is to enjoy Him and glorify Him forever.

Okay, that was a long way of saying that the Lord's Prayer course affected my life. During my stay at the hospital with Patrick during his heart surgery, I was at the point of learning about the line, "Give us this day our daily bread." I was learning to ask God about anything and everything in my life.

To understand this miracle, you need to understand that Patrick's surgery happened in Pittsburgh in 1978. Pittsburgh has been an industrial city from early days. At one point, it was considered the heart of the steel industry. The coal and steel industries, as well as many other large manufacturers, centered in Pittsburgh because of the rich coal seams nearby (as well as the confluence of rivers and good transportation). These manufacturers include Heinz, Alcoa, Iron City Beer, Joy Manufacturing, and many others. The point is that Pittsburgh has historically been a very industrial and polluted place. The coal and steel industry started to slide downward in the 1980's, but they were still going strong in 1978.

One morning, during my stay at UPMC Children's Hospital with Patrick, I walked a block to a restaurant to get some breakfast. When I walked out of the hospital, the smog hit me in the face like a ton of bricks. It made my nose burn and my eyes water. This was nearing autumn, and there had been a temperature inversion. (Here is an explanation of this from Wikipedia: "During an inversion warm air is above cooler air. An inversion traps air pollution, such as smog, close to the ground.") On my stroll to get breakfast, I passed a newspaper machine and stopped to look at the front page. The inversion was front page news, along with a warning to stay inside as much as possible.

As I walked, I pondered what I had been learning in relation to this inversion. I thought about each line of the Lord's prayer. I asked what God's will was in relation to the weather and the intense, resultant smog. The answer was perfectly clear to me. God does not want the earth and his people to be blanketed with this toxic fog. So, I prayed. Very simply. "Please God, take away this smog. In Jesus' name, Amen"

When I entered the restaurant, there was eye-burning, smelly smog. When I exited it with my fast-food breakfast biscuit, about 5 minutes later, the air was sparkling-clean, and the sky was crystal blue.

Job 12: 7-10 "But ask the animals, and they will teach you, or the birds in the sky, and they will tell you; or speak to the earth, and it will teach you, or let the fish in the sea inform you. Which of all these does not know that the hand of the Lord has done this? In his hand is the life of every creature and the breath of all mankind."

Thank You, Lord, for answered prayer and for tender mercies. Thank You for the very air that we breathe. In Jesus' name, Amen

No Coincidences (McLaughlin family story)

Admittedly, I brought the disaster in this tale upon myself, but it involved a miracle, nonetheless. After I had two separate breast cancers in my left breast, the medical people continued to find suspicious areas that looked like more breast cancers—not only in the left breast but also in the right one. This went on for many repeat visits, with lots of mammograms, repeated (higher resolution) mammograms, and close-together doctor visits. Finally, the doctors wanted to start the whole process over of doing another biopsy and another probable lumpectomy. At this point, my breasts already looked like they belonged to the bride of Frankenstein—there were so many scars from lumpectomies. (I had a total of four lumpectomies.)

You had better believe that all this testing and medical scrutiny was stressful to both my husband and me. Lee and I were basically never able to stop thinking about the threat of breast cancer, because it was constantly kept in front of our faces. Every time, there was another doctor visit or another test, our anxiety level would skyrocket.

Finally, at the point when they recommended another biopsy, I said, "I am done. Take them off." (Mastectomy is the medically recommended protocol when there have been two separate areas of cancer like I had.) My doctor apparently did not believe that I really wanted mastectomies, and he kept putting me off. He insisted that I have the biopsy, and I said that I wanted mastectomies, not another biopsy. We were at a standoff for about a month. Finally, I ended up in tears from all the constant stress while I was on the phone with my doctor's office. My surgeon finally seemed to understand what all this continuing drama was doing to me—he did the mastectomies. It turned out that the suspicious areas were non-cancerous.

Regarding the reconstruction choices, I blindly followed my doctor's advice, never even considering not having implants, I went ignorantly into getting them (first silicone, then later replaced with saline). Another mistake was taking the first available plastic surgeon, instead of researching for the best.

My plastic surgeon was not great at communicating. After I had my permanent implants in, he told me that I could do anything that I felt like doing. This was disastrous instruction for me, although it probably should have been common sense to take it easy after such a surgery. The thing that I did not consider was that the sensory nerves around my breast areas had been cut from all the surgeries. The pain that should have protected me from doing something stupid was not present. That fact, coupled with the bad advice from the plastic surgeon, as well as not using the commonsense God gave me led me to injure myself badly.

Right at the time of my implant process, our youngest son and his wife were moving into their first home. Foolishly, I went to help them clean before their furniture was moved there. I felt fine, energetic, and able to do the cleaning--so I did. At the end of the day, something felt very wrong on the left side. The area over the implant was hot, red, and quite swollen, plus I was in a boatload of pain.

Just as a sidenote, here is another thing that Lee and I learned the hard way. If you have a true emergency, get an ambulance to take you to the Emergency Room. Lee drove me, and as insistent as we were that I needed immediate attention, the girl at the desk (who looked like she was in high school) did not see it that way. I waited a good half-hour, if not more, pacing and moaning in pain. I learned later that a patient brought by ambulance gets immediate care.

Finally, the medical personnel took me back to a room. Here is the miracle. By this time, it was about 10:00 pm, and we were pretty sure that whatever doctor we might get would not know what to do about a breast implant problem. As arranged by our good Heavenly Father, an area plastic surgeon, Dr. T, was at the hospital checking on one of his patients. This doc was an excellent plastic surgeon, with a reputation for quality care. One of his areas of expertise was breast plastic surgery. He came to the Emergency Room to see if he could help me. (Remember, there are no coincidences, just God's orchestration!)

When Dr. T saw me, he knew immediately that I had ruptured my left pectoralis muscle which was stretched over the breast implant to hold it in place. He rushed me quickly into surgery. When he cut the area open, it spurted out over a pint of blood all over the place. He said my left pectoralis muscle looked like hamburger. The poor doc was worried he would lose me, so he had pictures taken to document it all to protect himself from liability. This kind, gentle and very skilled doctor saved my life.

Isaiah 41:10-12 "Do not fear, for I am with you; Do not anxiously look about you, for I am your God. I will strengthen you, surely, I will help you, Surely I will uphold you with My righteous right hand."

Thank You, Lord, for Your provision and miracles even when we have done something stupid. Thank You for putting Your helpers in the right place at the right time. In Jesus' name, Amen

Conclusions

Human beings are notorious for explaining away events in our lives as coincidences. Instead of seeing God's hand in an amazing intervention, we call it a happenstance.

What could be the result in our lives if we start recognizing non-coincidences? (For instance, when God places a person in just the right place at the right time to save a life like He did with the plastic surgeon for me. Or when he cleared out the smog in Pittsburgh in answer to a prayer.) Instead of being cynical, we should give thanks and pray for God's continued interventions.

Questions to ponder:

1. How many miracles have you written off as coincidences?
2. If you change your thinking to say there are no coincidences, might you better perceive the hand of God at work in your life?
3. Do you have a non-coincidence story to relate?

CHAPTER 6--MIRACLES OF ENCOURAGEMENT

Some people live through incredibly hard times. They can reach rock bottom but find reinforcement when they cry out to God for help. These stories show the tender heart of our God. Anyone who needs Him can have his supporting presence. Take in the details of how these brave individuals sought and received encouragement from our Father who cares.

God Speaks to Us in Mysterious Ways

This story happened about ten years ago to my niece, Ellen Shilling. Let me tell you a little bit about this sweet girl. Ellen has always had a special place in my heart because, as a young girl, she was such a nurturer. She was often carrying one of her younger siblings around on her hip, even though they were almost as big as she was.

A decade ago, Ellen gave birth to her son Jack, and not long afterwards she was diagnosed with Stage Four Hodgkin's Lymphoma. We have all heard that type of cancer is very treatable, but for a subset of people, it is not easily brought under control. Ellen was one of those individuals in the hard-to-heal group.

As Ellen went through treatment, things never seemed to go smoothly. If something could go wrong, it did. Before her protocol started, they put a port in to administer the chemo drugs. It did not function correctly—it turned out that the port itself was faulty. The medical staff had to do another surgery to remove it and insert another port.

Ellen went through the first four doses of chemo, followed up later by a scan to see if it worked. Not only did it not beat back the cancer, but the lymphoma grew (instead of shrinking) during the chemo.

They decided on another chemo regimen, one that is rarely used because it is extremely toxic. However, Ellen's lymphoma was so aggressive and advanced that the doctors chose this route. During the treatment, Ellen went to the emergency room twice with bone crushing pain all over her body. The drug used to boost white blood cell growth caused a rare side effect of causing off the chart bone pain. Every bone in Ellen's body felt like it was being smashed by elephants. At the emergency room, the administration of morphine did nothing to help. When they added Dilaudid (another morphine derivative), she finally got some relief.

Ellen had been going through each hurdle like a trooper, but one morning she reached her limit. She woke up feeling bad, so she checked her temperature. If she had a higher temp than 100.7 degrees, the doctor was to be notified. Ellen not only had a fever, but also it quickly skyrocketed. Andrew, Ellen's husband, rushed her to the emergency department. They knew right away from the doctors' reactions that it was very serious. A group of doctors was huddled around the monitor watching what was happening with Ellen's vital signs. Her blood pressure was bouncing all over the place. Ellen felt like she was dying and could only think of her son, Jack. She desperately wanted more time with him.

It turned out that Ellen was in septic shock from a urinary tract infection. Her immune system was so compromised that when the bacteria invaded her bladder, her body could not fight it off, and it became a whole-body infection.

Only about fifty percent of those who get septic shock recover. Those with abdominal sepsis, like Ellen's, have an even lower chance of making it—approximately twenty eight percent.

Ellen was kept in the Intensive Care Unit for a few days, and during that time they put in a central line. This was not even used, and they took it out a few days later. This was another trauma to her beleaguered body.

Ellen was shaken to the core by this last turn of events—she knew how close she came to dying. It was right before Christmas, and Ellen begged to be allowed to go home for the holidays. Amazingly, on December twenty third, Ellen got to go home to her family. As Andrew and Ellen were on their way back from the hospital, they passed a marquee of an old-fashioned movie theater. This movie house no longer functioned except for special events. On the sign above the ticket booth it said, "God Bless Us Everyone." Ellen saw this and knew it was a communication from God to her. It opened her eyes to look and listen to what He was saying.

Despite this ray of hope, Ellen had reached rock bottom. She had been undergoing treatment for one-and-one-half years and did not think she had more in her to keep going forward. Throughout the whole cancer experience Ellen had many conversations with God, but this evening's communication with Him, after her near-death experience was deeper--a turning point in her life.

Ellen went to the bathroom after arriving home and had a full-body, total, all-out cry—the kind that leaves you trembling and gasping for air. She felt completely broken as she poured out her heart to God, "I need a sign—I cannot keep doing this without You."

The next morning, she took her coffee and went to sit on the front porch, ignoring the December chill. A butterfly flew over and landed on her coffee mug. It just stayed there as Ellen processed the fact that God sent this beautiful creature to encourage her and to show her that He was with her. She was absolutely flooded with peace and knew without a doubt that she would be okay. (As an editorial question: how many butterflies have you seen at Christmastime in Pennsylvania? It does not happen!).

Here is the kicker—it was a monarch butterfly. They cannot live in the cold; therefore, they migrate to Mexico in early fall. That monarch was totally out of place for the season.

Ellen calls this her salvation moment. While she wanted to believe in her younger days, she had doubts and did not feel a personal connection with God. This one-to-one communication from God changed the way Ellen viewed the world. While she was always a positive person, she began to see everything as a blessing. Even the cancer! As a working woman, Ellen would have been back to work in twelve weeks. Because of her lymphoma, Ellen was home with her beautiful son, Jack, for his first two- and one-half years. She loved being with him in those crucial years.

Strangely, the more grateful Ellen and Andrew became, the more they were blessed. Ellen became adept at finding the blessing in every situation—her gratitude multiplied at every turn as she thanked God for her son, her husband and for each day of life. If she has an off-day or a sad moment, Ellen has learned to flip it by giving it over to God.

Now, Ellen is a woman of strong faith. Whereas church used to be something she endured, now she loves the hymns, the Bible, the fellowship, and the teaching. She feels that gathering with other believers renews her and keeps her spark from getting quenched. That is not to say that things are perfect, however throughout her life now, Ellen feels more connected and alive.

Another interesting change is that she does not believe in coincidences anymore. Ellen knows that everything that comes into her life is filtered through the hand of God, and she does not want to miss one thing that God has for her.

Okay, you thought this story was over, right? The hardest part was yet to come. The second, very harsh chemo protocol did not work either. Three months after treatment, the scan revealed that more drastic measures were needed.

A stem cell transplant was next on the agenda. This was unspeakably brutal, involving total body radiation and a two-day chemo regimen. For the transplant to work, there needed to be NED (No Evidence of Disease).

Ellen had ten days of inpatient pre-treatment to get ready for the procedure. The procedure itself was an autologous transfer, meaning they used Ellen's own stem cells taken from her bone marrow.

For Ellen, the hardest part took place next. Jack had to be taken to Andrew's parents' home for the next thirty days because Ellen would have zero immunity. Ellen remembers, with tears, the agony of leaving Jack. He must have sensed that it was for a longer than normal period because he was inconsolable--screaming and banging on the glass as she left. (For Ellen, being a mom supersedes everything else, so she recorded stories for Jack to hear her voice. She facetimed with him as much as she could, but she is quick to say that God got her through it. The other thing she did to deal with pain and what seemed to be never-ending procedures was to think of Jack. She would picture him playing or think of something he said. Such a great mom!

For the following thirty days, Ellen had to go to the hospital to be checked and get platelets or plasma as needed. The process went fairly well, but every few days Ellen would be admitted to the hospital because her blood counts were low. During this whole procedure, Ellen was unable to eat. She went from one hundred and fifty pounds to eighty-nine. She could not taste food, and as much as she tried, food just would not go down. Her doctor was sure that she would be all right, and after five weeks, she began eating again.

The stem cell transplant worked, and Ellen is okay (just as she knew she would be, after God sent his special butterfly sign). Ellen doesn't talk about it unless you ask her, but she is a quiet testament to God's goodness and love.

Ellen's response to the question, 'What are miracles?' was this: "Understanding God is far beyond our capacity. Yet, to me, our purpose here is simple—love God, love each other, and leave the world a better place. We are all very interconnected, and we are not fully able to comprehend that either."

"I needed my interaction with God when the butterfly made it's visit to me—it gave me a sense of total peace. That was my miracle. I was at rock-bottom, and God pulled me out of that."

Recently, I saw Ellen and wondered at the joy and peace that radiated from her. After hearing this story in its entirety, I understand the source of Ellen's glow.

Psalm 40: 1-5 "I waited patiently for the Lord; he turned to me and heard my cry. He lifted me out of the slimy pit, out of the mud and mire; he set my feet on a rock and gave me a firm place to stand. He put a new song in my mouth, a hymn of praise to our God. Many will see and fear and put their trust in the Lord. Blessed is the man who makes the Lord his trust, who does not look to the proud, to those who turn aside to false gods. Many, O Lord my God, are the wonders you have done. The things you planned for us no one can recount to you; were I to speak and tell of them, they would be too many to declare."

Father, thank You for pulling us out of the pit when we call
to You. Thank You for the gift of peace. Please give us all
hearts full of gratitude and recognition of blessings like
You did for Ellen. In Jesus' name, Amen

Dad and the Patriarch

In the last part of his life, my dad went through a time of
tremendous suffering. He was a very strong man, but the
agony that he experienced went way beyond what most
humans ever go through. You should know also that Dad
was the toughest man I have ever known, but even for him
the pain was too intense to be borne. Before this point, my
father was still extremely active and physical. He chain-
sawed down trees, split them, and sold firewood into his
eighties.

The problems all started when Dad began having angina.
He wrote it off to indigestion, but his doctor discovered
that he had heart blockage. The doc recommended that my
dad see a heart surgeon and have a cardiac bypass
procedure. Dad chose to have the surgery done by a local
cardiac surgeon whom his family doctor recommended.
(My dad's mistake was not listening to my brothers, who
said that we should look for the best in the nation and take
Dad there.)

Dad had the bypass done, and things seemed to be okay,
until Dad reported that his pain was increasing greatly, not
improving as it should have. He was not listened to by the
medical staff until it reached a crucial point of excruciating
agony.

Thankfully, I was spending the night at the hospital in
Dad's room at that critical juncture. In the wee hours of the
morning, I ended up screaming at a doctor who once again
was not taking Dad's pain seriously. I yelled, "Listen to my

dad because he is not a wimp! His pain is unbearable, and you all need to find out why it is getting worse and not improving."

This was the night before Easter Sunday, and finally, a team of doctors came in to examine Dad. They took him off for tests, and we waited anxious hours to hear the news. Early the next morning, we found out that Dad had a slashed intestine. The surgeon had nicked it with a scalpel when he did the cardiac bypass. Dad had fecal material in his chest cavity which caused his sternum (breastbone) to become infected. They had done emergency surgery during the night to remove his infected breastbone and clean out what they could of the feces spread throughout Dad's body.

Upon hearing the report in the morning, I was despondent and certain that we were losing Dad. Gary, my younger brother, and Rick, my middle brother, on the other hand had been talking to God--they both had a certainty that Dad would be okay. They were positive that, somehow, God had this well in hand. They were completely convinced that Dad would come through this with flying colors.

They were one hundred per cent right. The Holy Spirit had communicated to my brothers that God was taking care of this situation, which he did in ways we never imagined. During the emergency surgery, the doctors removed Dad's sternum. They cut a portion of his pectoral muscle, rolled it up and placed it into the space where my father's breastbone used to be. If they had not done this, Dad's heart would have been totally unprotected.

The battle was not over. Dad still had massive infection throughout his chest. Strangely, at the hospital where he was getting his care, they did not seem to treat this with the gravity it deserved. There was even talk at one point, very early-on, of sending him home, while he was still in this horrible state. My mother, a medical librarian, used her connections to tactfully pull strings without offending people. She got Dad transferred to another facility and placed under treatment of a caring woman-physician who was an infectious disease specialist.

This was the beginning of a long process of healing. There was immense sepsis that still had to be treated with multiple intravenous antibiotics. Dad was in the hospital for a grueling month—a long torturous time of tests, procedures, and various medical interventions. No matter how you cut it, it was pure hell that involved unimaginable pain and suffering.

Dad stood it all with grace and strength. He was always kind to the medical personnel, no matter what. I was in absolute awe of him. After it was all over, I asked him how he could possibly have endured all that he went through. In my thinking, he would say something like, "My family pulled me through."

What Dad told me left me completely dumbfounded. To understand my shock, know that my dad was totally pragmatic, never mystical in any way. Here is what he told me, "A patriarch came and sat silently by my bed in the hospital. I did not know who he was, maybe Abraham or Moses. He never spoke. I drew strength and hope just from him being there."

Here is the strangest part, we found out later when Dad went to Cleveland Clinic to be treated for another condition that the surgeon who did the bypass surgery did not correct his problem at all. The cardiac surgeon who performed Dad's surgery did not do the bypass that he was supposed to do. Amazingly, Dad never was bitter about this. He was able to keep his attitude of gratitude all the way to the end of his life.

Despite all the intense suffering that he went through, Dad had more years of love and life with us. Our family and many others counted themselves blessed to have Dad and his gentle influence continue in our lives.

Isaiah 43:2. "When you pass through the waters, I will be with you; and when you pass through the rivers, they will not sweep over you. When you walk through the fire, you will not be burned; the flames will not set you ablaze."

Thank You, God, for the gift of my wonderful dad and for
the miracle of giving us more years with him. In Jesus' name, Amen

Conclusions

God knows the power of encouragement. He sympathizes with our weakness and helps us when we need it. God can use a butterfly like he did for Ellen to help her stay the course. He can also send a patriarch to sit in silent support like he did for my dad.

It is so easy to give up, but God is there. Look for Him and His communications of love and tender care.

Questions to ponder:

1. Can you think of a time when you sorely needed encouragement and it was given? Can you relate a story?
2. Are there ways that you can provide encouragement to others? Can you be specific?

CHAPTER 7--MIRACLES OF GOD'S GIFTS

God loves to give good things to his children. Sometimes God knows the real desires of our hearts when we don't. Also, he often gives us what we need and not what we want. Relish these stories of God giving his kids the desires of their hearts.

Young Man at the Mall (McLaughlin family story)

When I was in my twenties, Lee and I went to a mall for a shopping mission. The mall was fairly crowded with virtually all the walkways filled with people. As we were walking along, I noticed there was an area in the crowd that was completely devoid of humanity. In the middle of this empty space, there was a young man walking towards us. His gait was normal, but his arms were making wild unpredictable motions in all directions (thus the empty space around him). Because of my physical therapy training, I recognized that this fellow had dyskinetic cerebral palsy (Also known as athetoid cerebral palsy.) This can be caused from trauma to a specific part of the brain during birth.

I looked at the young man just briefly then looked at all the people around him. The surrounding persons were all studiously avoiding giving any attention or eye contact to this gentleman. No one was looking in his face or acting like he even existed.

As my gaze returned to the young man, I saw something amazing. His face was vibrantly alive, with joy and light radiating from him. I was sure that it was Jesus that I saw glowing from his face. Our eyes met and there was a spirit-to-spirit contact when the Holy Spirit connected us. I smiled at him, and he absolutely beamed back. We did not speak any words and continued past each other. Yet, it was a moment that is emblazoned in my memory as significant and miraculous. (Lee did not notice the encounter but grasped the importance of it as I recounted the incident later.)

This young man needed a human connection—he needed to be seen, to be acknowledged, and to make a person-toperson contact. There is an old hymn that speaks of this type of God-created links with others, "Blest be the tie that binds our hearts in Christian love"[29]. The heavenly Father provided for this young man's need in that special moment, plus He blessed me profoundly as He did so.

Colossians 3:14: "And over all these virtues put on love, which binds them all together in perfect unity."

Thank You, Lord, for connections to others. Loving, in its many forms, is truly a gift and a miracle from You. In Jesus' name, Amen

Desires of Your Heart (McLaughlin family story)

Did you ever meet someone who was born to be a mother? Wendy, our daughter in law, is just such a woman. She is a nurturer, an encourager, and a total steel magnolia. She has her sweet southern accent and kindness that is unparalleled, but underneath she has a spine of pure steel that allows her to go the distance.

She is tiny but mighty, and if she decides on a certain path, then she talks to God and sets her eyes on the goal. Furthermore, she does it all with grace, never complaining or letting on to those around her of any hardships along the way. Wendy is one of my contemporary heroes—I often imitate her example of how to walk with Jesus. My oft-repeated prayer for her daughter, our granddaughter (Emerson), is that she will grow to be a godly woman of good and strong character like her mom.

Wendy will tell you that all three of her children are miracles, but this story is about getting our beloved twins, Emerson, and Knox, here to this earth. For whatever reason, Wendy could not get pregnant when she and Kevin were ready to have children. To have Cullen, they went the route of In Vitro Fertilization (IVF). It was a tough road, and I am sure that those who have never experienced it (including me) will not begin to understand the hardships. IVF makes you feel tumultuous with the overload of hormones, extremely emotional with the unknown outcomes, and left to function on zero energy. Just dealing with all the injections and even finding safe disposal for the needles is overwhelming. That said, our Wendy went through her first pregnancy with flying colors and gave us our precious Cullen. Obviously, Wendy's beleaguered body needed a break after having her first baby—essentially, she had been in a battle zone with the IVF. She needed to heal and gather her strength. This is not to minimize the hardship on Kevin—it was not a small task on his part either.

Yet, Wendy always knew she wanted more children, so before long they were trying again. Cullen's IVF had been a frozen embryo transfer, however using the same doctor and the same techniques was no longer effective to get Wendy pregnant.

Kevin and Wendy switched doctors and found one who seemed to understand their situation. He told her that she was thirty-two years old (but looked younger), however her ovaries acted like thirty-nine-year-old ovaries. This doctor was starting up an egg donor program and suggested that they use that, however Wendy and Kevin were not ready to go that route. Finally, the doctor pointblank told them that they would never have their own child—donor eggs were their only option. Heartbroken and weary in body and soul, Kevin and Wendy took a break and decided to focus on Cullen and the joy of having him in their lives.

In the meantime, I asked Wendy as often as I dared, to consider having a friend of mine, Mary Hamrick, pray for her to get pregnant. Wendy was resistant to this—she later told me that there is a shame associated with infertility that makes you want to hide. Finally, Wendy consented, and we went to the church where Mary and another friend prayed with her. I was not in the room with them, but I could picture it clearly when Wendy later described it to me.

Mary has a thing she does—she gets a certain look on her face, closes her eyes, and listens to the Holy Spirit. I don't know anyone who does it better. Often, she makes little "hmmm and mmm-hmmm" noises that I am sure she doesn't even know she is doing. Wendy told her story to these two prayer warriors and finished up by telling them what the doctor said about her not having any good eggs. Mary was doing her listening to Wendy while simultaneously hearing what God was saying. She finally said, "That is not true (about not having any good eggs). I am seeing two. Two eggs." They finished up the prayer time and Wendy thought to herself that it was nice, and she derived some comfort from it. But the 'two good eggs' part was filed in her brain as 'improbable'. Still, Wendy tucked the encouraging word away in her heart.

By this time, Wendy had undergone four IVF procedures using both fresh and frozen embryos. It is uncommon to have that many failures—Wendy sought out a website where other women were in the same situation. These ladies were saying that they were finally getting good results from the Colorado Center for Reproductive Medicine (CCRM). Wendy was hesitant to bring this up to Kevin because he was so burned out on doing IVF, nonetheless she brought it up at dinner one night. Kevin responded, "Let's do it!"

They flew as a family to Colorado, and friends out there took care of Cullen while Wendy went through six hours of testing. Another set of friends watched Cullen for the second trip out there. For the third trip, we brought Cullen for a visit to our farm. Wendy and Kevin felt so loved and rich in friends as their loved ones helped in any way possible.

Two days before Christmas, Wendy got the news that she was pregnant. The test for HCG was off the charts. Wendy asked the nurse who did the test if it was twins. She responded that if she were a betting woman, that would be her bet.

Wendy had a great pregnancy with twins, a boy and a girl—she was watched like a hawk because it was a high risk pregnancy. There was a concern that the baby girl was not getting her share of nutrition. (More on that later.)

When Wendy looked like she could not walk anymore because the babies were so big, they induced labor (but not because of her size). Knox was not as active as he had been previously, and the doctors were concerned so they scheduled the birth. They could see at the end of the pregnancy that Emerson was getting the nutrition that she needed, but because of an issue with the placenta, Knox was at risk. The little guy also had the cord wrapped around his neck when he was born. Emerson came out first, and all was fine with her. When Knox finally came out, there was no crying to signal that he was breathing and that all was well. The medical people hustled him off, and still there was no sound. Wendy kept asking "Is he all right?" but no one answered her. Just as she was really starting to panic, Knox started some lusty crying. The doctor came in the next day to discuss what happened and made the statement that Knox was lucky to be here. (By the way, Emerson was five pounds fifteen ounces, and Knox was five pounds twelve ounces. Both so little that you could hold each in just one hand.)

As a mother and grandmother, I know that Wendy has secretly watched Knox to make sure he is all right. He is completely okay— very active and sharp as a tack. He is a little chatterbox with a smile that could soften any heart. Emerson and Cullen are also equally charming, and they all bless our socks off. All three beautiful children were meant to be here, and Wendy and Kevin fought hard to make that happen.

Wendy says that she and Kevin were not without their struggles with God when pregnancy would not happen. Yet, knowing them both, I am sure they would have ended in a place of gratitude and devotion no matter the outcome. Wendy's view on miracles is, "Sometimes we need a big reminder that God is real and that he cares." Every time I look at those kids, I am reminded of how much he loves to give the desires of our heart to us.

Psalm 37: 4-5 "Delight yourself also in the Lord; and he shall give you the desires of your heart. Commit your way unto the Lord; trust also in him; and he shall bring it to pass."

Father God, you love to give us good things. Help us to have the determination to cooperate with You to bring the best possible things (or people) into our lives. In Jesus' name, Amen

Conclusions

God wants to give us the desires of our hearts. The Bible says that every good and perfect gift comes from the Lord.[30] A gift from God can be as small as a smile from a stranger and as huge as having children fill your home.

Questions to ponder:

1. Do you perceive God as the giver of good things?
2. Can you specifically point to a time when God gave you a desire of your heart? Could you share the story?

CHAPTER 8--MIRACLES OF GOD'S COMFORT

There are times when God just reaches out to offer us comfort. He is just that kind and loving. Sometimes we need to let our eyes and ears be opened to perceive and receive the comfort that God pours out upon us.

Lee's Mom (McLaughlin family story)

Lee's mom was an intelligent, well-educated, and inquisitive woman. Sadly, she developed dementia in her last years and went into a nursing home for care. Her decline was rapid in the sense that she lost memories, but she always seemed to know her loved ones at least to some level. She also retained her dignity to the very end.

Near the time that Alice died, Lee's and my prayers changed for her. We started praying for God to do what was best for her, even if that meant taking her home. It was not that we were ready to lose her—we were surprised ourselves that our prayers took that turn.

About a month after we started praying that way, I went by myself to Clemson University to visit our two youngest sons, who were in college there. The purpose was to do all the 'Mom stuff' that boys forget to do for themselves-like accumulated laundry, deep cleaning, and maintenance of the inside of their condo.

I was busy doing these things and enjoying time with Patrick and Kevin. Basically, at the end of a day, I would fall into bed and sleep like a rock because I was exhausted.

Near the end of the visit, I had one of my God dreams. It was very simple. Lee's mom was going through a doorway, dressed in a white suit, and she looked gorgeous. It was hard to tell how old she was in the dream-she seemed ageless, but not young. On the other side of the door she walked toward was a blinding light.

I called Lee the next morning and told him that his mom was going to die soon. That very day Alice went home to be with the Lord.

At the funeral, Alice was wearing the white suit of my dream. She also looked beautiful, timeless, and ageless. I noticed it, and others commented the same.

Revelation 21:4. "He will wipe away every tear from their eyes, and death shall be no more, neither shall there be mourning, nor crying, nor pain anymore, for the former things have passed away."

Thank You, God, for Your glimpses into what You have in store for those who call You Lord and Savior. In Jesus' name, Amen

Conclusions

Why does God give supernatural comfort periodically? Perhaps we are walking more closely with him in those intervals so that we have eyes to see and ears to hear. For whatever reason, God sometimes gives comfort beyond the ordinary. In my family's case the comfort was supernatural. A dream to show us that Lee's mom was going to a better place. Thanks to God for his tender nurturing and comfort.

Questions to ponder:

1. Have you ever needed God's special comfort to you?
2. Can you relate a specific story and the effects of God's tender mercies to you?

CHAPTER 9— *Miracles to Help us Grow in Character*

God uses circumstances in our lives to help us grow in character, or in other words to become more like Jesus. Cooperation is essential for this growing process to take place. Observe and learn from these real-life experiences

A New Man

How many people start off their new walk with God dealing with lots of dead bodies after a college shooting rampage? Scott Hayes did.

Scott's young years involved growing up with an alcoholic mom, and his early development was impacted by his mother's drinking (to the point that she passed out by dinner time every night). Scott was not exposed to Christianity while he was a child, with his first introduction to the church being when he dated, then became engaged to a Catholic woman. Scott obediently went through the Pre-Cana classes to get married in the church—he was still not a believer, but rather did what was needed to meet the requirements.

'A decent guy' was the label that Scott pinned on himself—he always filled his life with a lot of service. A life of helping had been modeled for him by his dad. He began his career as a doctor working in Family Medicine for sixteen years, plus doing emergency room part-time. This was rounded out by working as a random member on the rescue squad. Obviously, this left little time to be at home—he spent much more time with his work associates than with his family.

Eventually, Scott began to work full-time in the Emergency Department but continued with the rescue squads. Unfortunately, this put him in lots of situations where he was surrounded by bad influences. This group of rescue workers spent many hours away from home and there was a lot of moral decay in the field at that time. Scott succumbed to these influences and fell into sin.

There were terrible consequences—Scott's marriage split up. Scott carried a boatload of guilt—he knew that he had done wrong. For about two years, every day brought thoughts of suicide. Scott came close to carrying out his self-destructive thoughts by putting his truck in the garage to help him die by carbon monoxide poisoning. At this point, he went to a psychiatric hospital, knowing that if he did not get help, he would die. Through hours of classroom and group sessions Scott learned coping mechanisms and how to handle the guilt. Over and over a Higher Power was mentioned as a source of help. Scott knew that the God of the Bible was the Higher Power, and he knew that he needed to be in touch with God.

Upon being released from the Psych Hospital, Scott contacted his boss who pointed him to a church that was just starting up in Blacksburg, Virginia. Scott, with his sudden hunger to know God, started attending church and plowed through the Bible in six months. He began a Bible study with men at church doing R. C. Sproul's 'Dust to Glory' series of sixty DVD's surveying the Bible. As Scott read each section that Sproul talked about, he became awakened to the power of Christ, however, he had not crossed the line to become a believer yet.

Gary Abel, Scott's co-worker at the Emergency Department invited him to go on a 'Walk to Emmaus', and his boss seconded this suggestion. Here is a description of this three-day weekend from the 'Walk to Emmaus' website--"An experience of Christian spiritual renewal and formation that begins with a three-day short course in Christianity. It is an opportunity to meet Jesus Christ in a new way as God's grace and love is revealed to you through other believers. The objective of Emmaus is to inspire, challenge, and equip the local church members for Christian action in their homes, churches, communities, and places of work. Emmaus lifts up a way for our grace-filled lives to be lived and shared with others."

During the last session of the 'Walk', the attendees were encouraged to lay it all before God, repent, and give their lives to Christ. This was the first time that Scott understood what having a relationship with the God of the Universe through his son, Jesus Christ, was all about. He was on his knees--crying, repenting, and giving charge of his life to his rightful King.

Part of the weekend involved reading letters of encouragement from people in your life. Scott got many letters from people who had already seen a change in him as he searched to know God. The group then held hands and sang and began to dismiss for the weekend. A woman approached Scott and asked him to go on a medical mission trip to Nicaragua. Already Scott was starting to hear God's call for the things God had for him to do. Scott had found a new path—he had become a new man!

After the Walk to Emmaus, Scott had a restless Sunday night. He sat in his study and reflected on his notes from the long weekend.

Monday was supposed to be Scott's day off, but his boss called and told him that there had been some type of event on the Virginia Tech Campus. Scott's boss thought that Scott might be needed on the rescue squads. Scott called and arranged to meet an ambulance so he could help however he was needed. He called on his emergency walkie talkies to say that he was on his way to meet the ambulance. He was told that thirty to fifty people had died on campus and that they needed Scott to function as Medical Examiner. Currently there was no one else available. Scott changed plans to meet up with a policeman, who was in tactical uniform. They went to the Tech Campus to deal with bodies from the shooting spree that started in early morning.

Here is Wikipedia's description of the shooting.:

"It occurred on April 16, 2007, comprising two attacks on the campus of the Virginia Polytechnic Institute and State University in Blacksburg, Virginia. Seung-Hui Cho, an undergrad student of Korean descent, killed thirty-two people and wounded seventeen with two semi-automatic pistols. Six others were injured jumping out of windows to escape Cho."

"The first attack occurred at West Ambler Johnston Hall, a dormitory, where two people were killed; the main attack was at Norris Hall, a classroom building, where the rest of the lethal and non-lethal casualties took place in four classrooms and a stairwell. As police stormed Norris Hall, Cho fatally shot himself in the head. This remains the deadliest school shooting in U.S. history."

At the time that Scott was doing the job of medical examiner, little information was available as to what was happening overall. Scott knew that two people had been killed earlier in another building—police went to that area and left the academic area unprotected, which is where the bulk of the killing spree took place. The dorm shootings were just a diversion which drew the police there. Cho, the shooter, moved on to Norris Hall where he chained the doors shut and started shooting in a killing rampage.

This was the same place where Scott was working later. He was brought to Norris Hall to fill the position of medical examiner--his job was to get as much information as possible on the people who were killed: where they were in the room, identifications on them, etc. He was working amidst policemen, FBI agents, DEA agents, and another medical examiner technician--there were about thirty investigators working in the building. Known to these workers, but not the news media, was the added stress that Cho had said in a note that he also placed a bomb. These workers had that threat constantly hanging over their heads as they did their jobs. They tended to thirty-one bodies and worked from nine in the morning until about six in the evening. Scott was then relieved by the Chief Medical Examiner for Virginia who came in to take over.

At the end of his day, Scott had this thought, "God prepared me for this. He gave me peace to do what I had to do at this particular time."

With the danger of the bomb threat, Scott had the total surety that if he died, he would be with God. His strength to do the brutal job assigned to him came from giving his life to Christ.

Scott continues to get strength from Jesus. He is active in church, loves being in the worship band (playing bass) and does mission work. His spiritual hearing has been developed so that he perceives when God calls him to do something. He still loves to serve, and this has been a large part of his life with Christ. A cheerful giver, servant, and a behind-the-scenes type of guy, Scott has never been comfortable in the limelight. He has a quiet ministry for men in his home where he tries to create an atmosphere for them to be supported on their journey with God. Scott cheerfully cooks and gives encouragement freely. As a sidenote, he has a congenial relationship with his ex-wife, a close one with his kids, and he is happily remarried. The guilt and suicidal thoughts were left on the cross of Jesus, never to rear their ugly heads again.

2 Corinthians 5: 17 "Therefore, if anyone is in Christ, he is a new creation. The old has passed away; behold, the new has come."

Psalm 103: 8-12. "The Lord is merciful and gracious, slow to anger and abounding in steadfast love. He will not always chide, nor will he keep his anger forever. He does not deal with us according to our sins, nor repay us according to our iniquities. For as high as the heavens are above the earth, so great is his steadfast love toward those who fear him; as far as the east is from the west, so far does he remove our transgressions from us."

Father, thank You that we can become new. Our sins can be as far as the east from the west. We can learn to live new and purposeful lives in You. In Jesus name, Amen

Tearing Down My House with My Own Hands (McLaughlin family story)

Lee and I have gone through different stages in our marriage, and not all of these were beneficial or pretty. Both sets of our parents were good examples of sound marriage relationships, so we have no excuse for our actions. For some reason, in our early marriage, we thought it was okay to be competitive with each other-sometimes we were even harsh or critical. In full disclosure, I was much worse than Lee.

At some point in my late twenties, I read the verse Proverbs 14:1 "A wise woman builds her home, but a foolish woman tears it down with her own hands." I knew without a doubt that the Holy Spirit brought that verse to life for me. A light went on in my mind—I belatedly realized that every time I spoke negative words about Lee or any of my family, I was like the foolish woman in this verse. What I was doing by speaking anything critical of my family was tearing my house down with my own hands.

With God's help, I have changed this habit, for the most part. That alteration has brought about untold blessings. Lee and I now function more as a unit; he knows that he is respected and honored; and I am part of his cheering squad. The boys have my support instead of criticism. Where I thought I was helping by pointing out things that needed changing, I can now give positive reinforcement for the things that they do right.

If I see something of concern about Lee or my family, I take it to God. My prayer sounds something like this. "Hey God, Remember that child of yours, Lee McLaughlin. He is doing 'thus and so', and I don't think that is a very good idea. He is your child, God, so, I give him to you."

Hebrews 4: 12 "For the word of God is alive and active. Sharper than any double-edged sword, it penetrates even to dividing soul and spirit, joints and marrow; it judges the thoughts and attitudes of the heart."

Thank You, God, that with Your Word, with the Holy Spirit's help and with a choice on my part (which I must make repeatedly until it sticks), I can change. That is no small miracle. In Jesus name, Amen

Self-Hatred (McLaughlin family story)

In my early forties, my job was physical therapy, which, of course, was a hands-on profession. My hobbies involved doing various sorts of art (like oil painting and drawing) as well as many types of crafts (sewing, typing on the computer and such). Almost everything in my life required good hand dexterity.

Early on in my physical therapy career, I had treated a patient with Dupuytren's Contracture. Before he saw me, he had developed a completely non-functional hand-nothing that we tried physical therapy-wise helped it at all. Until I reached my fourth decade of life, seeing this patient was my only experience with this mysterious disease. Here is how it is described in Wikipedia, "Small, hard nodules develop just under the skin of the palm, then worsen over time until the fingers can no longer be straightened. While typically not painful, some aching or itching may be present. The ring finger followed by the little and middle fingers are most affected. This condition can interfere with activities such as preparing food and writing."

Even though I had seen this condition once before, I did not recognize it when it occurred in my right hand. I went to see a dermatologist who easily diagnosed it as Dupuytren's Contracture. He offered no treatment and told me a grim prognosis.

Of course, I called Lee on his cell phone to tell him what the doctor had said--I was extremely upset and crying. Poor Lee was driving at the time for his job, so he not only had to deal with all my drama but also had to navigate through traffic and manage work-related things.

After I unloaded on Lee, I went home from the doctor's office. The kids were not home from school yet, so I hopped on the treadmill and started talking to God. No, I began yelling at God!

"YOU DID THIS TO ME!! WHY WOULD YOU CAUSE THIS TO HAPPEN? WHY WOULD YOU ALLOW THIS TO OCCUR?"

I interspersed my yelling at God with messy crying jags that left tears and snot dripping onto the treadmill. This was a total-body, all-out, no-holds-barred conversation. Never did I have a talk with God like this one, and I never have since.

At some point, I was completely empty of all my emotions and words--I just continued to walk on the treadmill. Everything that I had to say to God had been said. The point had finally been reached that I could listen to what God had to say to me.

God did answer. His communication was so real that I thought that he spoke out loud. (Who knows whether he spoke audibly or in my head? I was the only one there.) Here was his response:

"Kathy, I did not do this to you. You did this to yourself. You hate yourself."

Shocker! Even more shocking was that when I called Lee afterwards to tell him about my conversation with God, he told me that he had been having his own talk with the Father, while driving. The Lord told Lee precisely the same thing—my self-hatred was causing my disease.

Something that I have never wanted to put out there in the public eye is that I learned later that my self-hatred stemmed from sexual abuse. (The reason I have kept this relatively private is that I did not want the pity or curiosity that would come with disclosure.) The abuse that I experienced was not the horrific, sustained major type you would imagine. I was French kissed and groped by an old man who probably had some degree of brain deterioration. I told my mom who gave me Listerine to wash out my mouth. She told this man in front of me that I was only to be kissed on the cheek. That should have been the end of it, right?

What I did not understand is that when a basic trust is betrayed in a young girl (or in an older one for that matter), there is lots of confusion and anger. Girls almost always turn those feelings inwards, because they don't know what else to do with it. They blame the betrayal on themselves (not consciously, but deep within their being).

Sometimes, the girl may bury the incident (or series of hurts) so deeply that she may not even remember it. To help them bury it, they may pile on pounds (to subconsciously protect themselves from inviting another wound by having a man want them). Alternatively, they may start cutting or stop eating because the anger turned inward becomes self-hatred. They may turn away from their normal attraction to boys, or they may become promiscuous. It is hard to predict what path a girl will take in her attempt to deal with the pain and anger. Usually, neither the girl nor their loved ones have any idea of the source from which this self-loathing and self-destructiveness arose. It does not seem to matter that the incident did not seem big enough to do damage or that abuse seems so immense that the girl could never heal. The resulting consequences are not necessarily proportional to the severity of the betrayal. (Boys with similar damaging experiences tend to turn their anger outward. That is a whole separate subject.)

Lee and I did not know at the point of discovering my self-hatred along with the Dupuytren's contracture that God would guide my best friend into finding Elijah House (An Inner Healing and Prayer Ministry). She and I would take classes, learn the teachings, and even become certified leaders. I would learn how to use the knowledge from the Bible and apply it to my life. Of course, there are other venues besides Elijah House to get to the root and heal the self-hatred from the inside out, but I don't personally know those.

Miraculously, I did stop hating myself and begin to understand at a heart level that I am God's own beloved daughter. This identity as God's beloved child is the only one that is not based upon me, on my relationships, on my own worth, or on my self-effort. It is the only identification that can never be taken away from me, no matter my circumstances. My identities of physical therapist, artist, author, daughter, wife, mother, or friend are vulnerable to change and loss.

As I grew in my heart knowledge of deep-healing truth from understanding and implementing the big principles of the Bible with the help of the Holy Spirit, the weapons of spiritual warfare became useful to me. Fending off lies from the enemy as well as accepting Truth became possible for me. (It is the truth with a capital T—Jesus— who sets us free.) Loving myself, plus helping others to gain the same perspective, became realities as I began to align myself more with Jesus's ways.

Dupuytren's Contracture never advanced further. It has been more than twenty-five years, and my hands have remained totally functional with good range of motion. I have the lumps in my right hand to remind me of God's miracle. They prompt me to do something else also—to hold loosely to things instead of grasping them selfishly. Along with understanding my self-loathing, I was given the impression that my greedy attitude was associated with my Dupuytren's contracture also. Because I was clutching onto things, it was showing up in my hand.

1 John 3:1 "See what great love the Father has lavished on us, that we should be called children of God! And that is what we are!"

Thank You, God for healing from the inside out—deep, miraculous healing. I am so grateful that You exposed the root of the problem and the solution. Thank You for giving

us great and unconditional love that can heal our self-hatred and the dis-ease that it causes. In Jesus' name,
Amen

Conclusions

What does it take to make us stop doing what we have always thought, said, and done? Sometimes we must get out of our comfort zone, out of our rut, or into some painful circumstances. Scott had the wisdom to seek wise counsel when his life fell apart. In my stories, I was willing to listen to God, to the Bible, and then to change. Can we grow without discomfort or pain? Possibly, some people can. I am one of the hardheaded ones who needs a severe jolt to change my trajectory.

Can we do anything to assist miracles coming into our lives? It is certain that we cannot manipulate God, however, we can keep a humble and God-honoring heart. God loves to be with people who enjoy his presence. Communing with Him opens that place where heaven and earth intersect. We can make a place for God in our souls and lives--inviting God to do life with us involves making stepwise choices that open us up to Him. Each choice either takes us closer to the Kingdom of God or further away—God loves obedience in thoughts, words, and actions. Another factor which aids in growing more perceptive of God is being bold and courageous in acting on our faith as well as persevering when times get tough. This can take us to a place where God can use us, and that is always a miracle. Choosing to watch for God-interventions can be an attitude that we cultivate; gratitude is certainly part of the right outlook. Lastly, as we get older, we can lose our sense of wonder and replace it with cynicism. Cynicism destroys the childlike view of the world that helps us to see miracles around us.

This book has given us some heroes to imitate, reminders that God cares, and next steps in moving forward in our relationship with the God of miracles (by emulating some of the characters in these stories). Even the smallest of these miracles shows God's willingness to come after us and pull us out of the mire and devastation of living in a fallen world.

The biggest miracle of all is God's overwhelming love and the ultimate sacrifice of Jesus to connect with us. We minimize that sacrifice of the cross because many of us have heard about it from the cradle, therefore we take it for granted. Nonetheless, the cross is our way to a relationship with the God of the Universe. Do not miss out on all that God has for you! He loves you beyond the truest love you have ever known.

The Lord told us in John 16:33, "I have told you these things, so that in me you may have peace. In this world you will have trouble. But take heart! I have overcome the world." We will not escape trouble, heartache, and hard times—that is part of life in a fallen world. Still, we can rejoice and celebrate that God is with us and is interacting with us. We can be forever grateful for having a God who sees, hears, and cares. We can remember the miracles, large and small, that our loving Father brings to us and revel in his great love.

Here are Jesus' own words about how to have Him manifested in our lives, "The one who obeys me is the one who loves me; and because he loves me, my Father will love him; and I will too, and I will reveal myself to him." John 14:21. Obedience to Jesus grows our love for Him, which leads to a loving relationship with the Father. This results in Jesus' love for us and His showing Himself to us (or making himself real in our lives.). Isn't that the true miracle that will last for eternity?

Father, help us to choose, love, and obey You. We want Your love, and we want to see You in our daily lives. In Jesus name, Amen

Questions to ponder:

1. Can you look back to events or epiphanies in your life that have brought growth in your character?
2. Do you think these times are usually tough or painful? Can you back up your answer with either scripture or your reasoning?
3. Can you relate a story of a time in your life that caused you to grow in character to be more like Jesus?
4. Do you recognize that while we are made in the God's image, we all have sinned and fall short of the glory of God? If not, are you willing to ask God to help you to see this from His point of view? (If so, just talk to God in simple words.)
5. Do you talk to God about the areas of your life that do not reflect Him and His glory? Repentance involves agreeing with God about the state of our hearts and lives then cooperating with Him to grow and change. Is that practice a part of your life? Could you talk about how you include this readjustment process in your daily walk with God?
6. Do you have anything to share about how this book has brought new thinking, words, or actions to your life?

Endnotes

1 Romans 8:28

2 Matthew 13:14-17, Ephesians 1:18

3 Matthew 6:33

4 Joshua 4:23-24, Deuteronomy 8:7-18, Acts 14:27

5 Isaiah 53

6 Acts 17:28

7 1 Corinthians 13:12

8 Psalm 145:9

9 Hebrews 1:3

10 Proverbs 18:24

11 From elijahhouse.org mission statement

12 Psalm 37:4

13 Ephesians 3:20

14 Philippians 3:14

15 Psalm 63:3

16 Malachi 2:16

17 Joshua 2:21, Joshua 2:18, Genesis 38:28, Genesis 38:30, Leviticus 14:6

18 Cory Asbury 19 2 Corinthians 3:16

[20] Oxford Dictionary

[21] Johns Hopkins Medicine

[22] Korean Journal of Neurotrauma. 2017 Oct; 13(2):63-67 Traumatic Cerebrospinal Fluid Leak: Diagnosis and Management, Ji-Woong Oh et al.

[23] The Lion, the Witch, and the Wardrobe

[24] 1 Kings 17:21-22

[25] Acts 20:10

[26] James 4:3

[27] John 2:24

[28] Acts 17:28

[29] "Blest Be the tie that Binds" by Reverend John Fawcett

Made in United States
Orlando, FL
13 March 2022

15729428R00148